Jan. 2016

Current
CONTROVERSIES

Professional Football

Other Books in the Current Controversies Series

Professional Football

Tamara Thompson, Book Editor

GREENHAVEN PRESS
A part of Gale, Cengage Learning

GALE
CENGAGE Learning·

Farmington Hills, Mich • San Francisco • New York • Waterville, Maine
Meriden, Conn • Mason, Ohio • Chicago

Judy Galens, *Manager, Frontlist Acquisitions*

© 2016 Greenhaven Press, a part of Gale, Cengage Learning

Gale and Greenhaven Press are registered trademarks used herein under license.

For more information, contact:
Greenhaven Press
27500 Drake Rd.
Farmington Hills, MI 48331-3535
Or you can visit our Internet site at gale.cengage.com

For product information and technology assistance, contact us at

Gale Customer Support, 1-800-877-4253
For permission to use material from this text or product, submit all requests online at
www.cengage.com/permissions

Further permissions questions can be emailed to permissionrequest@cengage.com

Articles in Greenhaven Press anthologies are often edited for length to meet page requirements. In addition, original titles of these works are changed to clearly present the main thesis and to explicitly indicate the author's opinion. Every effort is made to ensure that Greenhaven Press accurately reflects the original intent of the authors. Every effort has been made to trace the owners of copyrighted material.

Cover image Brocreative/Shutterstock.com

LIBRARY OF CONGRESS CATALOGING-IN-PUBLICATION DATA

Professional football / Tamara Thompson, book editor.
    pages cm. -- (Current controversies)
    Includes bibliographical references and index.
    ISBN 978-0-7377-7424-5 (hardcover) -- ISBN 978-0-7377-7425-2 (paperback)
    1. National Football League. 2. Football--United States. 3. Football--Social aspects--United States. I. Thompson, Tamara.
    GV955.5.N35P74 2015
    796.332'640973--dc23
                                                    2015021391

Printed in the United States of America
  1 2 3 4 5   19 18 17 16 15

Contents

Chapter 1: Why Has Professional Football Been in the News?

Even though it knew there was a scientific link between
brain damage and playing football, the National Football
League (NFL) tried to systematically thwart credible research and deliberately covered up the connection for
two decades.

A series of high-profile domestic abuse incidents among
professional football players in 2014 drew public attention to the issue of family violence in the National Football League, potentially undermining fan support for the
game.

Although the New England Patriots' ball-deflation cheating scandal grabbed headlines in 2015, it is just one in a
long line of cheating incidents that have besmirched the
integrity of professional football.

Members of the US Congress are urging the National
Football League to rename the Washington Redskins,
which Native American groups consider a racial slur and
have long fought to change.

The National Football League's new personal conduct policy is more about protecting the league's public image than getting tough on players who commit acts of domestic violence.

Professional football is the closest thing modern society has to ancient games of war and conflict; it allows fans and players to both express and sublimate their violent urges in a socially acceptable way.

Chapter 3: What Is the Impact of Drugs in Professional Football?

The National Football League fosters a culture where drugs are used and, often, overused to deal with the realities of ongoing pain and injuries suffered by players. While teams have improved their handling of drugs, especially painkillers, needed by players, the NFL still must implement better methods for dealing with the severe pain that players often endur as a result of playing football.

Marvin Washington, Brendon Ayanbadejo,
and Scott Fujita

The NFL should acknowledge the medicinal value of marijuana and fund research into its effect on brain injuries; players should be allowed to use marijuana for pain relief instead of prescription opioid painkillers, which have much more dangerous side effects.

Chapter 4: What Are Some Other Key Issues with Professional Football?

Jeff Nussbaum

The rules of professional football have been changed before to make the game safer and it worked. The NFL's rules and governance must again be adjusted to address the issue of brain injuries.

Yuval Rosenberg

The NFL is a multibillion dollar enterprise that has a vast impact on the US economy. From advertising and broadcasting to the sales of televisions and game-day snacks, to some 110,000 American jobs, football is good for the economy in many direct and indirect ways.

Alan Pyke

Hosting a Super Bowl is incredibly expensive and cities receive little return on their investment. Funding such events diverts money that should go to public safety, social services, and city jobs.

Foreword

By definition, controversies are "discussions of questions in which opposing opinions clash" (*Webster's Twentieth Century Dictionary Unabridged*). Few would deny that controversies are a pervasive part of the human condition and exist on virtually every level of human enterprise. Controversies transpire between individuals and among groups, within nations and between nations. Controversies supply the grist necessary for progress by providing challenges and challengers to the status quo. They also create atmospheres where strife and warfare can flourish. A world without controversies would be a peaceful world; but it also would be, by and large, static and prosaic.

The Series' Purpose

The purpose of the Current Controversies series is to explore many of the social, political, and economic controversies dominating the national and international scenes today. Titles selected for inclusion in the series are highly focused and specific. For example, from the larger category of criminal justice, Current Controversies deals with specific topics such as police brutality, gun control, white collar crime, and others. The debates in Current Controversies also are presented in a useful, timeless fashion. Articles and book excerpts included in each title are selected if they contribute valuable, long-range ideas to the overall debate. And wherever possible, current information is enhanced with historical documents and other relevant materials. Thus, while individual titles are current in focus, every effort is made to ensure that they will not become quickly outdated. Books in the Current Controversies series will remain important resources for librarians, teachers, and students for many years.

In addition to keeping the titles focused and specific, great care is taken in the editorial format of each book in the series. Book introductions and chapter prefaces are offered to provide background material for readers. Chapters are organized around several key questions that are answered with diverse opinions representing all points on the political spectrum. Materials in each chapter include opinions in which authors clearly disagree as well as alternative opinions in which authors may agree on a broader issue but disagree on the possible solutions. In this way, the content of each volume in Current Controversies mirrors the mosaic of opinions encountered in society. Readers will quickly realize that there are many viable answers to these complex issues. By questioning each author's conclusions, students and casual readers can begin to develop the critical thinking skills so important to evaluating opinionated material.

Current Controversies is also ideal for controlled research. Each anthology in the series is composed of primary sources taken from a wide gamut of informational categories including periodicals, newspapers, books, US and foreign government documents, and the publications of private and public organizations. Readers will find factual support for reports, debates, and research papers covering all areas of important issues. In addition, an annotated table of contents, an index, a book and periodical bibliography, and a list of organizations to contact are included in each book to expedite further research.

Perhaps more than ever before in history, people are confronted with diverse and contradictory information. During the Persian Gulf War, for example, the public was not only treated to minute-to-minute coverage of the war, it was also inundated with critiques of the coverage and countless analyses of the factors motivating US involvement. Being able to sort through the plethora of opinions accompanying today's major issues, and to draw one's own conclusions, can be a complicated and frustrating struggle. It is the editors' hope that Current Controversies will help readers with this struggle.

Introduction

*"Whatever the NFL empire has in store
in the coming years, one thing is certain:
Americans will be paying attention."*

If baseball is America's pastime, then football is definitely America's obsession. For thirty years running, professional football has been the country's most popular sport, but it became more than just a game a long time ago.

From the suspense and speculation of the preseason draft, to the glitz and glitter of the Super Bowl halftime shows, to the millions who play *Madden NFL* video games, pro football has transcended the world of sports to become the "most valuable entertainment commodity in the world"[1] and a cultural touchstone besides.

Comprised of thirty-two teams in two conferences—the American Football Conference (AFC) and the National Football Conference (NFC)—the National Football League (NFL) is the premier league for professional football in the United States. The teams each play sixteen regular-season games per year, followed by single-elimination playoffs that end with one team from each conference meeting in a championship game—the world-famous Super Bowl.

But the modern-day NFL barely resembles the professional football league that was founded in the 1920s, in an era when games were played for guts and glory, not multimillion dollar salaries and television market share. Pro football has long been popular, but the game has experienced a meteoric rise under the leadership of current NFL commissioner Roger Goodell, who since 2006 has taken a gritty and grueling sport

---

1. Steve Almond, *Against Football: One Fan's Reluctant Manifesto*, New York: Melville House, 2014, p. 84.

and repackaged it as a highly polished and exciting spectacle—with stunning results. According to a recent Adweek/Harris poll, almost two-thirds of all Americans watch NFL football—73 percent of men and 55 percent of women.[2]

Today's NFL is about much more than the game, however. The NFL is a multibillion-dollar sports-entertainment empire that manufactures and showcases elite athlete-celebrities whose personalities and personal lives are as much the story as their performances on the field. Exclusive NFL cable networks and original NFL programs feature exhaustive analysis of players and statistics to attract tens of millions of paying viewers each year. And slick promotion of routine league machinations creates a nearly year-round media presence that ensures football is never far from the public's mind.

Even the annual NFL players draft has been transformed from an internal meeting into a red-carpet affair, hosted live in prime time at world-famous entertainment venues, such as New York City's Radio City Music Hall. According to the NFL and Nielson ratings, the 2014 draft drew a record 45.7 million viewers.[3] As the Associated Press pointed out in 2014, "NFL officials are comfortable comparing the event to the Oscars or a big-budget movie premiere, as the league under commissioner Roger Goodell grows more aggressive in marketing an already wildly popular sport."[4]

Goodell's wall-to-wall strategy is clearly paying off: according to *Sports Business Journal*, the NFL's projected revenue for 2015 is $12 billion, roughly $1 billion more than the previous

2. Harris Interactive, "America's Sport—A Majority of Americans Watch NFL Football," harrisinteractive.com, October 14, 2011. www.harrisinteractive.com/NewsRoom /HarrisPolls/tabid/447/ctl/ReadCustom%20Default/mid/1508/ArticleId/880 /Default.aspx.

3. National Football League, "2014 NFL Draft Watched by a Record 45.7 Million Viewers," nfl.com, May 12, 2014. www.nfl.com/draft/story/0ap2000000349728/article/2014 -nfl-draft-watched-by-a-record-457-million-viewers.

4. Associated Press, "NFL Draft Goes for Glitz as It Moves to Prime Time," foxsports .com, June 2, 2014. www.foxsports.com/nfl/story/NFL-draft-goes-for-glitz-as-it -moves-to-prime-time-39561469.

year.[5] By *Forbes* reckoning, the teams themselves are worth more than $37 billion combined.[6]

While game ticket sales were the primary source of revenue for the NFL forty years ago, today they are believed to account for just 20 percent, with most of the league's profits now coming from broadcasting deals, media partnerships, merchandise sales, and various other initiatives.

Among the NFL's most lucrative deals: in 2011, the league signed broadcasting rights deals with four networks that together are worth $42 billion through 2022; the league's ubiquitous merchandising arm motivates Americans to spend more than $12 billion on NFL-branded clothing every year; and the *Madden NFL* video game franchise has sold more than one hundred million copies and generated over $4 billion in revenue to date.

And then there's the Super Bowl.

Web-based statistics company Statista estimated consumer spending on Super Bowl-related purchases would hit $14.31 billion in 2015, up nearly $2 billion from the year before.[7] But that's just part of the big game's impact.

Six of the seven most-watched television broadcasts in US history have been the last six Super Bowls, with the 2015 event drawing an audience of 114.4 million viewers, the largest of any TV show in history. With such unprecedented viewership, it's no wonder that a thirty-second Super Bowl ad spot sells for between $3.5 and $4 million.

But like the NFL itself, the Super Bowl is no longer just about the game. Super Bowl halftime shows and advertise-

---

5. Daniel Kaplan, "NFL Projecting Revenue Increase of $1B over 2014," *Sports Business Journal*, March 9, 2015. www.sportsbusinessdaily.com/Journal/Issues/2015/03/09/Leagues-and-Governing-Bodies/NFL-revenue.aspx?hl=2015%20nfl%20revenue&sc=0.

6. *Forbes*, "NFL Team Values: The Business of Football," forbes.com, August 2014. www.forbes.com/nfl-valuations/list.

7. Statista, "Estimated Super Bowl Related Consumer Spending in the U.S. from 2007 to 2015 (in Billion US Dollars)," Statista: The Statistics Portal, 2014. www.statista.com/statistics/217141/super-bowl-weekend-related-consumer-spending-in-the-us.

ments have become iconic cultural events in and of themselves, taking place on a global stage that has the power to make or break a music artist or consumer product in an instant. Because Americans don't just watch the Super Bowl; they talk about it. During the 2015 broadcast, viewers sent out more than 28.4 million tweets related to the game, ads, and halftime show, setting a new Twitter record.[8]

Football has always enjoyed a broad appeal that transcends demographics, and the ineffable way that it connects people and makes them feel like part of something bigger than themselves is perhaps the NFL's most valuable and enduring asset, especially now in the age of social media.

As longtime fan Steve Almond wrote in a recent critique of the game, "Given the game's appeal to traditional masculine values, it's hardly surprising that men of power gravitated to the game, nor that the ad executives of the world understood its lucrative associations. What remains shocking is the vast reach of the game, the manner in which it united low and high culture, the egghead and the meathead, the radical and the reactionary, the proletariat and the President."[9]

Indeed, football has become America's common denominator and the public's appetite for all things NFL appears insatiable. Commissioner Goodell is counting on exactly that as he strives to reach his goal of increasing annual revenue to a staggering $25 billion by 2027.

If the explosive growth in the NFL's popularity—and its business acumen—over the past decade are any indication of what is yet to come, Goodell may well succeed. Whatever the NFL empire has in store in the coming years, one thing is certain: Americans will be paying attention.

8. Brian Poliakoff, "The New England @Patriots #SB49 Win Plays Out on Twitter," blog.twitter.com, February 2, 2015. https://blog.twitter.com/2015/the-new-england-patriots-sb49-win-plays-out-on-twitter.

9. Steve Almond, op. cit., p. 18.

The authors in *Current Controversies: Professional Football* explore the current landscape of the NFL and examine some of the sport's darker aspects as well, including the impact of concussions, drug use in the NFL, and the question of whether football promotes violence.

CHAPTER 1

Why Has Professional Football Been in the News?

Chapter Preface

Although the National Football League (NFL) enjoys un-precedented media exposure that is overwhelmingly positive, not all of the press coverage is favorable to the league. To say that the NFL has had a rough couple of years in the public eye would be an understatement.

Beginning in 2014, the NFL absorbed hits from multiple directions as a seemingly endless stream of negative headlines cycled through the nation's press. Among the disclosures: several high-profile domestic abuse cases involving prominent players (the Associated Press named domestic violence in the NFL the nation's top sports story in 2014); concerns about player safety amid revelations that the NFL suppressed information about the devastating effects of repeated concussions (a lawsuit and settlement ensued); the April 2015 murder conviction of New England Patriots' tight end Aaron Hernandez; a federal drug probe into whether NFL team doctors and trainers illegally medicate players with powerful prescription painkillers; a lawsuit by cheerleaders alleging unfair labor practices and inadequate pay; a heated public debate over whether the league's nonprofit status should be revoked; continuing controversy over team names that Native Americans consider disparaging; a cheating scandal involving intentionally deflated footballs in the 2015 American Football Conference (AFC) championship game; and the list goes on.

The NFL has weathered bad publicity before. The infamous O.J. Simpson murder trial in 1995, the imprisonment of then-Atlanta Falcons quarterback Michael Vick for dog fighting and animal cruelty in 2007, and the New Orleans Saints' "Bountygate" scandal, in which players received bonuses for injuring opponents from 2009 to 2011, are just a few of the incidents that come to mind. But never before has the league faced so much simultaneous scrutiny from so many diverse quarters.

A great deal of sports desk ink has been spilled lamenting the NFL's "nightmare year" and the soul searching that the league and its fans have been forced to undertake on the horns of so many ethical dilemmas. Indeed, entire books have been written about whether continuing to support pro football is even ethical (most notably, Steve Almond's *Against Football: One Fan's Reluctant Manifesto*). But in the end, all the talk seems to matter very little.

"Despite all the NFL's self-inflicted wounds, the league actually got more popular this year," wrote Ed Sherman at the National Sports Journalism Center in February 2015.[1] "Yes, it couldn't have been worse for the NFL off the field this year. And what was the end result? The NFL scored some of its best ratings ever."

In fact, the 2015 Super Bowl set another all-time record with an audience of 114.4 million viewers, while "the NFL playoffs were at their highest levels since the '90s, as were several regular-season games."

"There might be outrage on the studio shows and sports talk radio about the NFL's declining standards, but it all gets shelved when the teams line up on game day," Sherman continued. "If the past season said one thing, it doesn't matter what happens to the NFL off the field. People still want to watch their games. The game has become too big to fail."[2]

The authors in this chapter discuss the issues that have put professional football in the headlines lately and consider the ramifications of those events.

---

1. Ed Sherman, "NFL Is Teflon: Ratings Soar Despite Nightmare Year Off-Field," National Sports Journalism Center, February 2, 2015. http://sportsjournalism.org/sports-media-news/nfl-is-teflon-ratings-soar-despite-nightmare-year-off-field.

2. Ibid.

NFL Concussion Revelations Heighten Concern About Game Safety

Don Van Natta Jr.

Pulitzer Prize-winning journalist Don Van Natta Jr. is a senior writer at ESPN The Magazine *and* ESPN.com. *He is the author of three books, including* First Off the Tee: Presidential Hackers, Duffers, and Cheaters from Taft to Bush.

The National Football League (NFL) conducted a two-decade campaign to deny a growing body of scientific research that showed a link between playing football and brain damage, according to a new book co-authored by a pair of ESPN investigative reporters.

The book *League of Denial: The NFL, Concussions and the Battle for Truth*, reports that the NFL used its power and resources to discredit independent scientists and their work; that the league cited research data that minimized the dangers of concussions while emphasizing the league's own flawed research; and that league executives employed an aggressive public relations strategy designed to keep the public unaware of what league executives really knew about the effects of playing the game. *ESPN The Magazine* and *Sports Illustrated* published book excerpts on Wednesday morning [October 2, 2013].

Head-On Collision

An excerpt from *League of Denial: The NFL, Concussions and the Battle for Truth* appears in the Oct. 14, [2013] edition of *ESPN The Magazine*, which is available on newsstands Friday [October 4, 2013].

The NFL's whitewash of the debilitating neurological effects of playing football suffered by players began under former commissioner Paul Tagliabue, who left office in 2006, but continued under his successor, current commissioner Roger Goodell, according to the book written by ESPN investigative reporters Mark Fainaru-Wada and Steve Fainaru.

The book, which will be released Tuesday by Crown Archetype, compares the NFL's two decades of actions on health and safety to that of Big Tobacco—the group of cigarette-making corporations whose executives for years covered up the fact their products contained dangerous, addictive, potentially deadly and cancer-causing chemicals.

"There are many differences," the Fainaru brothers write in *League of Denial* "but one is that football's health crisis featured not millions of anonymous victims but very public figures whose grotesque demises seemed almost impossible to reconcile with their personas."

A lawsuit filed against the NFL by more than 4,500 ex-players . . . charged that the league's Mild Traumatic Brain Injury Committee conducted fraudulent research to hide the connection between football and brain damage.

NFL executives declined to cooperate with the authors on the book. On Wednesday morning, league spokesman Greg Aiello declined to comment.

Major Findings

Among the major findings in *League of Denial*, which the Fainarus spent more than a year researching and writing:

- Two original members of a concussion committee established by Tagliabue disavowed the committee's major findings, including the NFL's assertion that concussions were minor injuries that never led to long-term brain injury.

- As far back as 1999, the NFL's retirement board paid more than $2 million in disability payments to former players after concluding football gave them brain damage. But it would be nearly a decade before league executives would publicly acknowledge a link.

- Beginning in 2000, some of the country's top neuroscientists warned the NFL that football led to higher rates of depression, memory loss, dementia and brain damage.

- The league in 2005 tried unsuccessfully to have medical journals retract the published work of several independent concussion researchers.

- Independent researchers directly warned Goodell about the connection between football and brain damage in 2007, but the commissioner waited nearly three years to acknowledge the link and to dismantle the league's discredited concussion committee. In 2009, two other independent researchers delivered still more evidence that football caused brain damage during a private meeting at the NFL's Park Avenue headquarters. Yet the league committee's co-chairman, Dr. Ira Casson, mocked and challenged the researchers so aggressively that he offended others who were present, including a Columbia University suicide expert and a U.S. Army colonel who directed the Defense and Veterans Brain Injury Center.

- As the crisis escalated, the NFL tried desperately to regain control of the issue and contain damage to its brand. Before an October 2009 hearing on football and brain injuries conducted by the House Judiciary Committee, the NFL lobbied successfully to prevent Goodell from testifying on the same panel as the father of a high school quarterback who had died after sustaining a concussion.

- Dr. Ann McKee, the leading expert on football and brain damage, told the authors that she believes the incidences of neurodegenerative disease among NFL players will prove to be "shockingly high" and that "most NFL players are going to get this. It's just a question of degree." Since 2005, when the disease was first diagnosed in deceased NFL players, McKee has studied 54 brains harvested from deceased NFL players. All but two had chronic traumatic encephalopathy (CTE). "I'm really wondering where this stops," she told the Fainarus. "I'm really wondering if every single football player doesn't have this."

Players File Suit

The health of former players and the league's previous scientific exploration formed the basis of a lawsuit filed against the NFL by more than 4,500 ex-players. The players charged that the league's Mild Traumatic Brain Injury Committee conducted fraudulent research to hide the connection between football and brain damage. On Aug. 29, the NFL and the former players settled the lawsuit for $765 million.

Former longtime New York Jets defensive lineman Marty Lyons, who is being inducted into the team's Ring of Honor on Oct. 13, was asked Wednesday about the issue of whether the league downplayed the concussion issue.

"I'm not going to accuse the league. You'd come off to the sideline [during a game] and maybe they wouldn't use the words 'You got a concussion.' You got dinged. Many times, they'd say, 'How many fingers?' You'd say three, and they'd say, 'Yeah, that's close enough' and you'd go back in," Lyons told ESPNNewYork.com's Rich Cimini. "That was by choice. That wasn't doctors or trainers saying, 'You're OK.' They would tell you to sit on one side of the bench and they would go look at other players. Next thing you'd know, you'd be back out there on the field. Players had to be more responsible for their own actions. I'm not saying the league didn't know, I'm not saying the players didn't know. It was part of the game."

One of the most significant findings in the book, for which the authors say they conducted more than 200 interviews and reviewed thousands of pages of previously undisclosed documents, traces how the league handled research under Tagliabue's guidance.

Industry-Funded Research

In 1994, Tagliabue established the Mild Traumatic Brain Injury [MTBI] Committee to act as the league's concussions investigatory committee. According to the book, the committee published its controversial research in a medical journal, "Neurosurgery," that was edited by a consultant to the New York Giants. The Fainarus write that the consultant, USC [University of Southern California] neurosurgeon Dr. Michael Apuzzo, was a "sports guy wannabe" who frequently worked into conversations that he'd just had lunch with Tagliabue and was thrilled to stand on the sidelines during games.

[Current NFL commissioner Roger] Goodell inherited a concussion mess from [Paul] Tagliabue but ... Goodell took nearly three years to acknowledge a link and moved slowly to publicly address the growing crisis.

Some of the studies the NFL had published in "Neurosurgery" had startling conclusions: Concussions were minor injuries; multiple concussions did not increase the risk of further injury; and football did not cause brain damage. "Professional football players do not sustain frequent repetitive blows to the brain on a regular basis," the NFL's doctors asserted, according to the book.

Often, the Fainarus write, Apuzzo ignored peer-reviewers' objections to the league research before rubber-stamping it into the journal. The actions led some concussion researchers to privately ridicule "Neurosurgery" as "The Official Medical Journal of the National Football League" and the "Journal of No NFL Concussions," the authors write. Apuzzo declined to be interviewed for the book; he also declined to be interviewed for this story.

Dr. Kevin Guskiewicz, a researcher who joined the league's new concussion committee after the NFL dismantled the MTBI group, rejected the "Neurosurgery" papers, which he described as "industry-funded research at its best," according to the book.

Sharp Criticism

Dr. Mark Lovell, who directed the NFL's Neuropsychological Program for 16 years, told the book's authors that concussion committee leaders inserted provocative language in research papers after they had been read and approved by other members, including him. In one passage, Lovell called "stupid" a claim by league researchers that it was "unlikely that athletes who rise to the level of the NFL are concussion prone." He also said he did not write that sentence. When the Fainarus reminded Lovell that he was listed as an author, he replied: "No, no, no. I mean, is my name on that sentence?"

The book levels sharp criticism at the handling of the health and safety issue by Goodell, who succeeded Tagliabue in August 2006. The authors write that Goodell inherited a concussion mess from Tagliabue but that Goodell took nearly three years to acknowledge a link and moved slowly to publicly address the growing crisis.

The book also does not spare independent concussion researchers. The Fainarus write of conflicts of interest, eccentricities and ego clashes among the independent researchers who wanted a piece of the concussion research. What emerges is a tale of researchers seeking to be part of a morbid brain chase, the prize of which is not only medical prestige but also money in the form of millions of dollars in donations and grants for continued research.

Under Goodell, the NFL has been a major contributor to funding such research. In 2010, the NFL gave Boston University [BU] $1 million and designated the university's Center for the Study of Traumatic Encephalopathy as the league's preferred brain bank. The league also pledged to encourage retired players to donate their brains to BU. But in 2012, four months after the suicide of former San Diego Chargers linebacker Junior Seau, and after multiple former players had been diagnosed posthumously with CTE by Boston University researchers, the league distanced itself from BU and donated $30 million to the National Institutes of Health.

Cherry-Picked Researchers

The book also describes how the league intervened in the scramble among researchers on who would be chosen to study Seau's brain, which would ultimately be diagnosed with CTE by the National Institutes of Health.

By relying on interviews, documents and private emails, the Fainarus describe the extent to which independent researchers felt pressured and harassed by the league. A neuropathologist named Ron Hamilton said the NFL attempted "to set up a barrier," to let "everybody know that [we] were just insane." Steve DeKosky, one of the nation's leading Alzheimer's experts, wrote in a private email to his colleagues that the NFL was "stunning in its hypocrisy."

The book also relates the story of Mike Webster, the ex-Pittsburgh Steelers center and member of Hall of Fame who was the first NFL player to be diagnosed with CTE. In the final years of his life, Webster frantically accumulated an arsenal of weapons and had seriously considered turning them on

NFL officials, whom he blamed for his deteriorating mental condition, Webster's son told the authors.

"No Revenge, No Sir," Webster wrote in a rambling letter to his family not long before his death in 2002. "Not Revenge, But *Reckoning*."

Adrian Peterson and the Sport Fan's New Quandary: Watch or Not?

Patrik Jonsson

Patrik Jonsson is a staff writer for the Christian Science Monitor.

The indictment for child abuse of one of the NFL's best players, Minnesota Vikings running back Adrian Peterson, hit an already reeling world of sports on Saturday, raising a stark question: What's a fan to do when some athletes' values fall so far out of step with their own?

The allegations against Mr. Peterson—that he seriously injured his 4-year-old son, in what Peterson called a "normal whooping"—comes after the country cringed at video footage of now-former Baltimore Ravens running back Ray Rice coldcocking his wife-to-be in a New Jersey casino. Simultaneously, the NBA's [National Basketball Association] Atlanta Hawks had to deal with a series of racist remarks from its owner and general manager, and, in what became almost a footnote, Dallas Cowboys owner Jerry Jones was slapped with a sexual assault charge, which he has denied.

As a result, fans were forced to take notice of "the most controversial week in sports history," as the *Boston Globe*'s Jeremy Gottlieb called it.

To be sure, athletes and league bosses acting badly or, worse, breaking the law is hardly eye-opening anymore. It's also true that today's media often flourishes on manufactured outrage.

Moreover, there has been some sympathy for players laboring under over-sized expectations that take a heavy toll on their bodies and their minds. In Baltimore, both male and female fans were seen wearing Rice jerseys this week, presumably in solidarity with the indefinitely suspended player.

But this week's litany of family violence in the homes of fabulously-paid athletes has given at least some fans pause about how Sunday afternoon pastimes seem to have careened fundamentally out of step with some of the country's most cherished values, including protecting one's family from harm.

Indeed, the situation has given rare pause to some fans about their own role in the dead-serious dramas playing out in the media.

"[W]hat's a sports fan to do?" wonders Mashable's Sam Laird. "If you're like me, your sports addiction runs way too deep to give up now.... In the short term, however, I probably won't watch much—if any—NFL this weekend. Instead, I'll go outside. Feel the sun on my face. Enjoy the breeze. Lay in the grass. Maybe join a pickup basketball game—the kind of break from ugly reality that being a sports fan used to provide."

Previous doping and drug-abuse scandals in sports were serious and leagues took action, but were ultimately ignored or downplayed by many fans. The more recent domestic abuse allegations—underscored by video, in the case of Rice, and pictures, in the case of Peterson's son—seem to have struck a more profound note.

The confluence of perverse behavior—much of which was uncovered by media operations far out of the sports mainstream—has shaken the league-fan partnership.

"Physical abuse of women or children is completely unacceptable ... but something about [what Peterson is alleged to have done] is absolutely sickening, reprehensible and unforgivable," writes Patrick Rishe, a sports economist at Webster University, in St. Louis, on *Forbes.*

The "whooping" with a tree branch switch, police say, happened in May [2014], in Spring, Texas, after Peterson's son had tussled with another of his children over a video game. The beating, police say, caused several injuries to the boy, including cuts and bruises all over his back, buttocks and legs. There were also defensive wounds on the child's hands, doctors testified.

Peterson's attorney said Friday that Peterson was employing the kind of discipline imposed on him as a child. "Adrian is a loving father ... [and] it is important to remember that Adrian never intended to harm his son and deeply regrets the unintentional injury," the lawyer said.

To be sure, a lot of American fans will tune out the news and tune into the games this weekend. But it's also clear that the confluence of perverse behavior—much of which was uncovered by media operations far out of the sports mainstream—has shaken the league-fan partnership.

Indeed, allegations of spousal and child abuse—and concerns about whether sports leagues are in turn serious about punishing top athletes in their playing prime with possible career-ending suspensions—have pushed the sports fan quandary to a new level, some sports columnists argue.

So far, two other NFL players involved in domestic abuse allegations—[San Francisco] 49ers' Ray McDonald and Carolina Panthers' Greg Hardy—have been allowed to continue playing until their court cases are settled.

After Friday's indictment, the Vikings have pulled the prolific Peterson from the Sunday lineup, which will make it hard for the team to beat the New England Patriots. Fans will likely watch carefully how the NFL treats the allegations. Traditionally, the league has waited for court cases to be settled before taking action, but it's sure to come under intense pressure to deal with Peterson more immediately, especially after the Rice debacle.

"[Roger] Goodell, the embattled commissioner, should call an emergency midweek timeout, summon every player in the NFL to Chicago or Dallas on Tuesday, the players' day off, and hold a seminar with lectures by experts in anger management, domestic violence, child abuse, drug abuse and every other abuse their players are capable of performing," writes Gary Myers, in the *New York Daily News*. "Then Goodell should emphasize that it's a privilege, not a right, to play in the league."

Through his career, Peterson, a former MVP, has rushed for 10,190 yards and 86 touchdowns through six years in the league. His home life has been plagued with trouble. As a child, Peterson watched a drunk driver kill his brother, Brian, who was riding his bike; his half-brother, Chris Paris, was shot and killed in Houston, in 2007; and last year, a 2-year-old son Peterson barely knew, Tyrese Ruffin, was killed by the boy's mother's boyfriend.

Cheating Scandals Have Tarnished Pro Football's Reputation

David Fleming

David Fleming is a senior writer for ESPN The Magazine *and has penned the popular "FlemFile" column for ESPN.com since 1996. He is the author of* Breaker Boys, *a book about the still-controversial 1925 National Football League title game.*

In my search for answers and understanding regarding the cheating scandals in New England and, really, in every other inch of our modern sports landscape, the most shrewd and succinct explanation I came across was provided by none other than the [New England] Patriots' owner himself, Robert Kraft.

In the 2012 book *Coaching Confidential: Inside the Fraternity of NFL Coaches* by Gary Myers, Kraft explained to readers just how thoroughly humiliated he was by the 2007 Spygate taping scandal. With good reason. The illegal taping scheme that involved an assistant spying on the New York Jets' defensive signals resulted in a record $500,000 fine for coach Bill Belichick (a punishment that now seems laughably light), the forfeiture of a first-round draft pick, and a lasting smudge on what is otherwise one of the most dominant and successful franchises in sports history.

In the book, Kraft first exhausts what sociologists might categorize as a textbook list of excuses for people caught red-handed. "How much do you think that helped us?" Kraft wonders, rhetorically. Then later, "You know how many teams steal signals?" After his attempts to minimize and deflect fall short, the Patriots' owner says he finally decided to confront Belichick about the illegal taping.

This is how it went:

"How much did this help us on a scale of 1 to 100?" Kraft says he asked Belichick.

"One," Belichick replied.

"Then you're a real schmuck," Kraft told Belichick.

Bingo.

Well, the schmuck is back, or so it appears.

"Deflategate"

This week [January 2015], according to league sources, the NFL [National Football League] found that 11 of the 12 footballs used by the Patriots in a 45-7 win over the [Indianapolis] Colts in the [2015] AFC [American Football Conference] Championship Game were significantly underinflated. A move, I suppose, that was meant to give the Patriots an advantage in a game they probably could have won using just 10 players on a side while spotting the Colts a touchdown, or two. Still, if it's true, this latest accusation of cheating (and make no doubt, that's exactly what it is) is the epitome of paranoia, insecurity and arrogance—and while the crime seems silly, the punishment should not be. There have been so many bizarre scandals with this franchise, moving forward we should just start referring to them as the New England Gatetriots.

It's a schmuck smorgasbord out there, people, and it just goes on and on.

Sadly, though, the Gatetriots are just another reminder of two of the larger truths in sports: Cheating is no longer the exception, it's the rule. And Kraft had it 100 percent correct. The absolute worst thing about these cheating scandals is

"The Wizard of Oz" effect—the way they reduce our sports heroes, our sports dynasties, and the rest of us, too, into little more than sports schmucks.

You see, cheating doesn't distinguish Belichick. It actually does something much more damaging to his legacy: It makes him pedestrian—nervous, paranoid and full of self-doubt like a little boy, just like every other schmuck out there.

Take a quick look around: It's a schmuck smorgasbord out there, people, and it just goes on and on, a beacon of insecurity and corner cutting emanating from Foxborough [Massachusetts] and radiating out across the entire sports world.

Cheating Is Cheating

There's so much cheating going on, in fact, that I had to consciously narrow the focus of this column—no steroids, no PEDs [performance-enhancing drugs], no point shaving, no bounty scandals, no fake classes or illegal payments to college kids. There simply isn't enough time or bandwidth to cover it all here. And I, for one, am tired of all the rationalizing. Spying on opponents or deflating footballs isn't gamesmanship or pushing the envelope, and it doesn't fall under the ignorant NASCAR [National Association for Stock Car Auto Racing] creed of, "If you ain't cheating, you ain't trying."

It's cheating. And the schmucks who do it are as old and as widespread as sports itself.

Fred Lorz won the 1904 Olympic marathon by riding in the backseat of a car for around 11 miles (he was disqualified). Olympic figure skating had Tonya Harding [who had her opponent assaulted]. Little League baseball had Danny Almonte [who was two years older than the league allowed].

The 2000 Spanish Paralympic team used a dozen or so ringers. Seriously, they did that. They faked disabilities to win a medal. (Feel free to abandon all hope.) And then there's my personal fave: There was so much cheating going on in the

Big Bass Classic during the mid-1980s that one of the winners confessed to never having even baited a hook.

[In baseball,] there's Sammy Sosa's corked bat. Joe Niekro's emery board. Michael Pineda's pine tar.

[In hockey,] Marty McSorley's curved stick that may have changed the outcome of the 1993 Stanley Cup.

How many injuries have defenders faked to try slowing down the [Philadelphia] Eagles' offense? How many wrecks in NASCAR are premeditated?

The "Schmuck Factor"

Yet, why a three-time Super Bowl champion like Belichick would even consider cheating is the reason we're all so transfixed by these scandals to begin with. It's the Schmuck Factor. We're transfixed by cheating in sports because we're never closer to our heroes than when—driven by the same insecurities, self-doubt and pressures that plague us all—even the great ones are reduced to cheating to try to find an advantage.

Think about it: Big bad untouchable genius Bill Belichick, gazing out from under his hoodie like Darth Sidious? Turns out he's as scared and unsure as, well, every other coach, athlete or human being who came before him.

Belichick grew up in the shadow of his father, Steve Belichick, who spent three decades as a renowned and respected assistant coach at the Naval Academy. In 1975, the son wanted so badly to follow in his hero's footsteps that he started out as a gofer working for the Colts for $25 a week.

"Never Again"

Twenty years later, I stood next to Bill, then the head coach of the [Cleveland] Browns (but not for long), under the bleachers of Cleveland Municipal Stadium as angry fans mocked him with chants of "BILL MUST GO! BILL MUST GO!" Belichick had a scrunched, indignant sneer on his face that couldn't quite mask all the fear and disappointment he felt at having failed as a coach, as a man, and maybe, he thought, as a son, too. Never again, you could sense him thinking. Never again. No matter what it takes. Never again. I'll never be in this position again. I will never be made to feel this way again. No matter what I have to do.

I hadn't seen that look on his face for 20 years. But when reporters bombard Belichick with inquiries about the Patriots' latest scandal, my guess is you'll see that face once again, that thinly disguised sneer—the worry, deep down, that after all the wins and all the championships, maybe Robert Kraft was right.

If the Patriots win a fourth Super Bowl [they did in February 2015] and Belichick is found to have cheated his way to the Lombardi [Trophy], once again, he will likely go down in history, twice.

As the game's best coach.

And, just another in a long line of cheating sports schmucks.

Editor's Note: On May 6, 2015, the National Football League (NFL) released its final report on the New England Patriots' ball-deflation cheating scandal, finding it was "more probable than not" that team employees deflated footballs used by the Patriots' offense in the January 2015 American Football Conference (AFC) title game against the Indianapolis Colts and that star quarterback Tom Brady "was at least generally aware" of the arrangement. The 243-page report did not find any evidence that coach Bill Belichick knew about the scheme. The NFL later announced penalties that included a four-game suspension for Brady, a $1 million fine for the team (matching the largest in league history), and forfeiture of the Patriots' first-round draft pick in 2016 and fourth-round pick in 2017. Two equipment staffers for the team were also suspended indefinitely. Brady vowed to appeal.

Washington, DC, Team Faces Pressure to Change Derogatory Name

Travis Waldron

Travis Waldron is a reporter and blogger for ThinkProgress.org at the Center for American Progress Action Fund, a progressive public policy research and advocacy organization.

Fifty United States Senators have called for a change to change the name of the Washington Redskins in a letter to National Football League [NFL] commissioner Roger Goodell released Thursday [May 22, 2014]. The letter, first reported by the *New York Times*, cites the NBA's [National Basketball Association] swift action against the racism of Los Angeles Clippers owner Donald Sterling and asks Goodell and the NFL to take similar action against a name Native American activists call a "dictionary-defined slur."

The letter echoes the remarks Senate Majority Leader Harry Reid (D-NV) made on the Senate floor immediately after the NBA announced that it would ban Sterling, who made racist comments about African Americans, for life and would seek to force a sale of the team.

"Today, we urge you and the National Football League to send the same clear message as the NBA did: that racism and bigotry have no place in professional sports. It's time for the NFL to endorse a name change for the Washington, D.C. football team," the letter states.

"Now is the time for the NFL to act," it continues. "What message does it send to punish slurs against African Americans while endorsing slurs against Native Americans?"

Only five Democrats—Virginia Sens. Mark Warner and Tim Kaine, Indiana Sen. Joe Donnelly, West Virginia Sen. Joe Manchin, and Arkansas Sen. Mark Pryor—did not sign the letter. Kaine and Warner's absences are notable, as both represent the state in which the team is based.

A Majority Signs On

The 50 signatures mean that a majority of the U.S. Senate has now spoken out against the name. Arizona Sen. John McCain (R) did not sign the letter, which the *Times* said was not circulated among Republicans, but challenged its continued use in the wake of the Sterling ban. "If they think it's that offensive and terrible, I would certainly—probably—I'm not the owner and he has the rights of an owner. But frankly I would probably change the name," McCain said during an appearance on *The Dan Patrick Show* earlier this month. "Myself I'm not offended. You're not offended. But there are Native Americans who are."

This is the third letter from Senate and congressional leaders to the NFL in the last year. Reps. Tom Cole (R-OK) and Betty McCollum (D-MN), co-chairs of the Congressional Native American Caucus, and eight other members of Congress sent a letter demanding a change to the NFL in May 2013. Cole and Sen. Maria Cantwell (D-WA), the former chair of the Senate Indian Affairs Committee, sent a similar letter to the league in February [2014]. President [Barack] Obama is on record saying he would consider changing the team's name, and other congressional leaders, including House Minority Leader Nancy Pelosi (D-CA), have called on the team to drop the name.

The Oneida Indian Nation of New York, which has led a public campaign against the name since the beginning of the 2013 NFL season and National Congress of American Indians (NCAI), which has opposed the name for more than 50 years, "applauded" the letter in a statement.

Name Is "Offensive and Hurtful"

"The name of Washington's NFL team is widely recognized as a racial slur," NCAI executive director Jackie Plata said in the statement. "The NFL is a global brand, but if it wants to contribute to the positive image of the United States across the world, rather than callously promoting discrimination against Native Americans, then it must stop promoting this slur and finally change the name."

"The R-word is a dictionary defined racial slur, which likely explains why avowed segregationist George Preston Marshall decided to use the term as the team's name," Oneida representative Ray Halbritter said. "Continuing an infamous segregationist's legacy by promoting such a slur is not an honor, as Mr. [Daniel] Snyder [Washington Redskins team owner] and Mr. Goodell claim. It is a malicious insult. That is why leaders in the Senate, in the House of Representatives, in the White House, and at all levels of government across the country are uniting in opposition to this offensive and hurtful name."

Pressure from the federal government is not new for the Washington Redskins. In the 1960s, the team became last in the NFL to integrate its roster only because the [John F.] Kennedy administration threatened to deny the team the use of Washington's RFK Stadium until it signed a black player.

NFL Cheerleaders Take the Spotlight with Lawsuits over Fair Pay

Howard Bloom

Howard Bloom contributes to Sporting News *and is the long-time publisher of* Sports Business News, *an online newsletter that focuses on the relationship between sports and business.*

In the midst of the greatest image crisis in recent NFL [National Football League] history, the optics of which are in part focused on the relationship the NFL has with women, how the league treats its cheerleaders, long viewed as eye-candy at NFL games, is in the news.

Twenty-six of the 32 current NFL franchises have cheerleading teams, with the Baltimore Colts becoming the first in 1954 and the Dallas Cowboys later pushing the cheerleaders' ability to influence ticket sales.

But as much as they are valued as a business bonus, cheerleaders have for the most part received little more than recognition for the hundreds of hours they put into their game day preparation, performances, and the many different events they attend on behalf of the NFL teams they represent.

The Raiderettes last week [September 2014] were awarded a $1.25 million settlement on back wages owed to members of the [Oakland] Raiders cheerleading team. Under the terms of their previous agreement, the cheerleaders made less than $5 an hour. Under their new agreement, they will be paid $9 an hour. Four NFL teams (Cincinnati [Bengals], Buffalo [Bills], Tampa Bay [Buccaneers] and New York [Jets]) are still dealing with cheerleader-related lawsuits.

The Bengals, Buccaneers and Jets all have cheerleading teams, but the Bills disbanded the Jills in May after the Jills filed their lawsuit. When the Bills play the Dolphins in Buffalo's home opener Sunday [September 14, 2014], it will be for the first time since 1967 without the Jills.

In their filing, Buffalo's cheerleaders contend they were asked to work 16 hours or more during the NFL season and for all of their efforts, were given a parking pass to Ralph Wilson Stadium. The Ben-Gals were paid $45 a game, well below minimum wage when the hours of unpaid practice time is factored in.

Woman and the NFL Experience

How the NFL values women will be at the forefront of the looming court cases. According to *Bloomberg BusinessWeek*, based on New York's $8 hourly minimum wage, factoring in the 20 hours each Buffalo Bills cheerleader had to invest once they were selected as a Buffalo Jill for the 42 weeks of their cheerleading season (tryouts, practices, regular season and playoff games), the Bills would have to invest $235,000 for the entire Jills squad.

It seems almost morally reprehensible that the NFL is allowed to treat cheerleaders as badly as they have, while simultaneously trying to sell a message of inclusion for women fans.

Cheerleaders have become a fundamental part of the NFL's game day experience. With the average NFL ticket price nearly $85 this year, it seems incomprehensible NFL teams would continue to pay cheerleaders next to nothing for the entertainment they offer NFL fans.

How often are cheerleaders on camera as part of the NFL's $4.9 billion network agreement? According to Eric Smallwood, an analyst at Front Row Marketing Services, a Philadelphia-based company that consults with sports teams on sponsor-ships, the answer is an average of seven seconds during most broadcasts—more often than not on the way to and from commercial breaks. That represents $317,000 per year for each of the 26 teams with cheerleading squads last season.

How important are cheerleaders to the Atlanta Falcons? At the start of the 2014 season, the Falcons introduced a new in-centive for returning season ticket holders. Fans have a chance to order a seat-side visit from a pair of Atlanta Falcons cheer-leaders.

It seems almost morally reprehensible that the NFL is al-lowed to treat cheerleaders as badly as they have, while simul-taneously trying to sell a message of inclusion for women fans.

Pro Football's Legal Issues Attract Government Scrutiny

Kaveh Waddell

Kaveh Waddell is a staff correspondent for National Journal, *where he previously conducted policy research.*

In recent months, politics and American football have been clashing increasingly often. Congress and the [President Barack] Obama administration have found themselves on the opposite side from the NFL [National Football League] over issues ranging from health concerns and doping to a team's racist name and the league's nonprofit status.

President Obama is the most recent entrant to the fray. Following a smattering of comments over the course of the two years that hinted at his concern over concussions in football, Obama brought together leaders of national sports leagues at the White House on Thursday [May 29, 2014] for a Healthy Kids and Safe Sports Concussion Summit. At the event, the president announced numerous partnerships with sports organizations, including a $30 million program in conjunction with the NCAA [National Collegiate Athletic Association] and the Defense Department for concussion education, and a $25 million pledge from the NFL to fund a variety of strategies to reduce concussion rates. While the conference focused on the safety of young people, the NFL could be worried that future generations of pro football players (or their parents) might shy away from the sport in favor of safer pastimes.

Obama has remarked on safety in football before. Last year [2013], he told *The New Republic,* "I think that those of us who love the sport are going to have to wrestle with the fact that it will probably change gradually to try to reduce some of the violence." In a conversation with *The New Yorker* in January of this year, Obama said outright, "I would not let my son play pro football."

The complaints over safety aren't coming out of nowhere. In August 2013, under national scrutiny, the NFL settled a lawsuit brought against it by former players for $765 million. The sum will be applied toward medical exams and research, litigation expenses, and compensation for affected players.

Months after the lawsuit settled, Sen. Tom Coburn, R-Okla., introduced a bill to strip the NFL of its nonprofit status. Under current law, the league is exempt from taxes because it qualifies as a 501(c)(6) organization along with "business leagues, chambers of commerce, real estate boards, and boards of trade," according to the IRS [Internal Revenue Service]. A feature in *The Atlantic* outlined the big-ticket costs that NFL teams pass on to taxpayers.

Most recently, the football team in Washington [DC] has been under fire for refusing to change a name that is a racist slur. A band of 50 Democratic senators came together to sign a letter sponsored by Sen. Maria Cantwell, D-Wash., urging the commissioner of the NFL, Roger Goodell, to throw his weight behind a name change for the team.

On Thursday, the NFL tried to strike back with an ill-fated Twitter campaign. The official account of the Washington football team tweeted an attempt to rally support behind its name and send a clear message to Senate Majority Leader Harry Reid, D-Nev.:

"Tweet @SenatorReid to show your #Redskins Pride and tell him what the team means to you."

ThinkProgress compiled some of the fallout that the communications team behind the tweet may not have anticipated, made up of replies that ranged from "obstinate ignorance" to "overt racism."

Once an escape from politics, football—the most popular sport in the U.S. for the 30th year running—is becoming increasingly tangled up with a Congress suffering from record-breaking low approval ratings. The pace only seems to be increasing: The government and the NFL may remain strange bedfellows for some time.

CHAPTER 2

Does Professional Football Perpetuate Violence?

Overview: Boxing Fell from Favour as We Became Less Tolerant of Violence. Will American Football Follow?

Ed Smith

Ed Smith is a British journalist and author of the book Luck: What It Means and Why It Matters. *A former professional cricket player, he writes a weekly column for the* New Statesman, *a weekly British political and cultural magazine.*

When Joe Louis fought Max Schmeling in 1938, two-thirds of Americans tuned in to the radio broadcast. Now, most sports fans can't tell you who the current heavyweight champion is without recourse to the internet. I can't, either, though I used to follow boxing closely. Tastes change. Boxing never had to be abolished. Betrayed by bad governance and marginalised by increased intolerance of violence (notwithstanding the very occasional big night), it has been quietly pushed off centre stage. Will American football—the favourite sport of the US, as well as a patriotic showcase and the preferred vehicle for big business interests and mass media—go the same way as boxing?

American football is a brutal game: intense physicality courses through its veins. Recently, I stood on the touchline of the MetLife Stadium in New Jersey watching the New York Jets play the Chicago Bears. From the distance of a few feet, I saw men the size of small trucks charging, marauding and careening towards each other. The collisions were seismic: enormously muscled players, psychologically wound up like coiled springs, intent on imposing their physical dominance.

I have watched many cricket balls, intended to hit me, go past my nose at 90 miles per hour. Yet I gained a new insight into sport's primal DNA in just a few moments ringside at an American football game.

The fury of the NFL lies in its capacity to combine the brevity and intensity of sprinting with the aggressive intent of boxing. A boxer seeks to hit his opponents on the head, whether scoring punches or knockout blows. Other games demand that violence be abstracted; boxing leaves the darkness pure. Yet a boxer must also evade and endure, over as many as 12 rounds of three minutes. Boxers must be endurance athletes as well as fighters. Each of them, to a greater or lesser degree, blends defence and attack.

Sprinters—although there is no physical contact, let alone confrontation—hone their bodies and minds to operate at the limit of their primal instincts. A sprinter worships explosiveness and hones his fast-twitch muscles, training himself to the full extent of fight-or-flight capacity. Sprinting takes an evolutionary trait and exposes it to cutting-edge science. Where boxing is violence tempered by time and endurance, sprinting isolates explosive power and aggression while divorcing them from violent ambition.

The financial imperatives that encourage clubs to forgive erring star players at the peak of their career are the same ones that discourage investigation of injuries that could blight them in their retirement.

The NFL mixes these two elements to create a compound effect: explosive violence. A typical play lasts only a few seconds, often less. Years of mental and physical conditioning are expressed in a moment of urgent destructiveness. That's why, for all its tactical sophistication and abundant skill, the NFL boils down sport to its primal residue.

These facts are not new. But other, more disturbing facts are now interacting with football's underlying rhythms. First and most troubling is brain damage. According to the *New York Times*, the NFL concedes that it expects nearly a third of retired players to develop "long-term cognitive problems". Three years ago, the former player Dave Duerson killed himself with a shot to the chest. He was 50 and suffering from chronic traumatic encephalopathy, causing dementia and depression. He hoped to leave his brain in one piece so that his decline could be examined and explained.

Off-field crises proliferate. The celebrated running back Ray Rice was videoed punching and knocking out his fiancée (now his wife) in a lift. He was initially suspended for two games, which became an indefinite suspension when the video became public. Child abuse charges have been initiated against Adrian Peterson, another running back, after he allegedly beat his four-year-old son with a tree branch. He was first cleared to play, before being forced to miss all his matches until the case has been heard.

Logically, intrinsic on-field health risks should be unconnected to a string of off-field scandals. Yet, in reality, the two subjects are intertwined, as the financial imperatives that encourage clubs to forgive erring star players at the peak of their career are the same ones that discourage investigation of injuries that could blight them in their retirement. The more general question is reinforced: just what kind of sport is this?

The NFL has introduced a raft of safety measures. It is now illegal to tackle or charge leading with the crown of the helmet; a neuro-trauma consultant must be present at every match; teams are allowed only one full-contact practice session per day; there is a campaign at youth level to educate players about safety, as well as a $60m programme to develop diagnostic technology.

As an ex-sportsman, I will always defend people's right—and sometimes need—to take risks. But American football, so strong as a corporate machine, is engaged in unprecedented soul-searching. Barack Obama has said that if he had a son, "I would not let [him] play pro football." Many of us who love rugby union feel something similar.

Obama's comment was braver than it sounds to English ears. American football remains the sport of the US establishment. When I discussed Obama's opinion with Troy Vincent, until recently a star player and now a senior executive at the NFL, he replied with lightness and mischief but also with an underlying seriousness: "That's one less player for my boys to get past!"

Will American football go the same way as boxing? "Without being prideful, I can't see that happening. Football is strong. Players are much more educated on these issues around safety," he added. His final, rousing comment was this: "[American football] is not going anywhere!" But in 2014, something indefinable gave way in the great American love affair with the NFL. Vincent may be right but not necessarily in the way he intended.

Domestic Violence Is a Serious Problem in the NFL

David Leonard and Monica Casper

David Leonard is a regular contributor to The Feminist Wire *and other publications and is the author of several books, including* After Artest: The NBA and the Assault on Blackness. *Monica Casper heads the gender and women's studies department at the University of Arizona, where she is also a professor. She is the managing coeditor of* The Feminist Wire, *an online publication.*

The National Intimate Partner and Sexual Violence Survey found that fully a third of women in the United States have experienced partner violence. Authors of the study note that the long-term consequences and public health burdens are "substantial," especially for women. And yet, while many feminist groups continue to attend to these concerns and to seek redress for victims, intimate partner violence has receded from public attention since the 1970s, when the women's movement made it a major focus. Despite the statistics, domestic violence (or DV, as some activists call it) is often portrayed as a historical artifact rather than a persistent ugly crime.

Enter Ray Rice, Janay Palmer Rice, and the NFL [National Football League]. For months, the media and general public have speculated on "mitigating circumstances" to explain why [Baltimore Ravens running-back] Ray Rice knocked [his fiancée, now wife] Janay Palmer unconscious and dragged her crumpled body out of an elevator [in February 2014]. Mitigating circumstances ... a not so subtle way of blaming the victim.

Today [September 2014], with the release of the horrific video in which we see Rice coldcock his fiancé, we see once again that the system, from TMZ to ESPN, from the sports media to the legal system and the public at large, cares little for Janay Rice. It cares little about her desires, her voice, her body, and her victimization. "No one cares that she is now going to have to relive this incident over and over again. No one cares that the world has now become privy to what may be the most humiliating moment of her entire life," notes [political sportswriter] Dave Zirin. "No one cares that she's basically now being used as a soapbox with otherwise apolitical NFL commentators using her prone body to get on their high horse and blast the league. There is video and those who never raised their voice publicly about the axis of domestic violence and the NFL before are the loudest shouters now."

How Many?

How many NFL officials and players have thought about the hopes and dreams of Janay Rice? How many people, who excused Ray Rice throughout the summer only to feign outrage and shock today, continue to erase her humanity? How many radio hosts and articles, tweeters and online commentators, continue to reduce her to an object to be consumed, shared, and gawked at with the help of TMZ.

And if they really cared, where were they over the summer; where have they been in each and every case of domestic violence within the NFL; where have they been when activists have demanded that they participate in the Purple Ribbon campaign to raise awareness of domestic violence? Where have NFL officials and pundits been when women assaulted by their partners face severe traumatic brain injury—an issue about which the NFL claims to care deeply? As sociologists Dan Morrison and Monica J. Casper ask, "What we are not paying attention to when we focus our lens predominately on male victims of TBI [traumatic brain injury], such as combat veterans and football players, and the need for better protective gear? What of the silent epidemic of domestic violence in the United States, through which women suffer high rates of traumatic brain injury?"

Forgive us as we roll our eyes at any moral posturing from those very people who actively sanction a culture of violence.

Profits over People

The Ravens deserve NO praise for releasing Rice today, as its members spent months dismissing the seriousness of the situation. Whether they saw the video before today is irrelevant given a summer of denial. "It's not a big deal, it's just part of the process," Coach [John] Harbaugh told ESPN over the summer. "There are consequences when you make a mistake like that. I stand behind Ray. He's a heck of a guy. He's done everything right since. He makes a mistake, allright? He's going to have to pay a consequence. I think that's good for kids to understand it works that way. That's how it works, that's how it should be." One has to wonder what message Harbaugh thought he was sending to *girls* throughout the nation, when he describes the brutal assault on a woman as "no big deal." What sort of message was sent to Rice and countless other boys and men about what those consequences should be?

The NFL has some serious soul searching to do regarding not just its failures with Ray Rice, but with a culture that profits from violence, on and off the field. As of 2012, 21 teams had a player on its roster who had faced domestic violence or assault charges. Many of the men faced no real consequences. It is abundantly clear, over and over again, that profits takes precedence over people behind the NFL Shield, as evidence by the organization's prioritizing of the game and the business of the NFL, concerns that are advanced well ahead of Janay Rice and justice, every single time.

The Ravens and the NFL are not alone, as the prosecutor also has a lot to account for in this case. The prosecutor offered Rice the ability to participate in New Jersey's pretrial intervention program (PTI). Supposedly this decision was reached "after careful consideration of the information contained in Mr. Rice's application in light of all of the facts gathered during the investigation." What facts? What information? Is it the same sort of information that has anchored a culture that seemingly normalizes and accepts domestic violence? Is it more of "domestic violence is a private matter?"—which is very nineteenth century. Tell us what sort of facts, and while you are at, how might you clarify whether or not the NFL was given the tape. Because right now, it is hard not to see this case as yet another moment where the power structure goes to every length to protect and serve patriarchy.

A Symbol of Systemic Injustice

In a nation where 24 people experience intimate partner violence every minute, most of them women, Ray Rice is a mere microcosm of a larger systemic injustice. In a nation where 1 in 4 women report intimate partner violence, there are many more Janay Rices than we can even imagine (for more devastating facts, see the work of Soraya Chemaly). In a nation where 138 GOP [Grand Old Party, Republican] members of Congress voted *against* reauthorizing the Violence Against Women Act, forgive us as we roll our eyes at any moral posturing from those very people who actively sanction a culture of violence. In a nation where most incidents of domestic violence go unreported and where women are punished, sometimes by death, when they finally gather up the courage to leave an abusive partner, it should surprise nobody how much has been done to victimize Janay Rice over and over again, despite her heartbreaking and unnecessary apology for "the role that she played" in the incident.

According to [feminist critic] Soraya Chemaly, "The number one cause of death for African American women ages 15–34 according to the American Bar Association: homicide at the hands of a partner." It's bigger than Ray Rice; it's bigger than the NFL and the Ravens. This is about patriarchy and masculinity; it's about those who cite "mitigating circumstances," who blame the victim, who justify "boys will be boys," who systemically detract from the deadly issue of domestic violence. "But in a world in which one in four women [a recent survey reveals a number closer to 1 and 3] is the victim of intimate partner violence and black women are disproportionately targeted, this victim blaming is not just irresponsible; it is lethal," writes [black feminist writer] Hannah Giorgis. "Black women are punished when attempting to defend themselves: 94% of black female homicide victims are killed by people they know and 64% of those victims are wives, ex-wives or girlfriends of their killers."

Demanding Accountability

Ray Rice might be our current poster child, a symbol that allows the NFL to distance itself from domestic violence. But this is about a culture that, again and again, shows us that women's lives, and especially Black Women's lives, don't matter. To stand up and say enough, to demand not only justice for Janay Rice, but accountability from the Ravens, the NFL, ESPN, and so many others, is to assert that the lives of women, the lives of black women, matter. As Hannah Giorgis asks, "Who will support victims when abuse is not recorded and pre-packaged solely for our consumption but subtle and drawn out, or when the state itself commits violence?"

And who will demand justice and accountability from Ray Rice, but also from those who provide the oxygen and nourishment that allows domestic violence to live and flourish?

Who will challenge a culture of excuse-making that both blames and victimizes all too many women? Who will support Janay Rice and so many others, because we have seen enough?

NFL Players Face Token League Censure for Violent Off-Field Behavior

Travis Waldron

Travis Waldron is a reporter and blogger for ThinkProgress.org at the Center for American Progress Action Fund, a progressive public policy research and advocacy organization.

The National Football League's (NFL) owners ratified a new personal conduct policy Wednesday afternoon [December 10, 2014], and it took league representatives less than an hour to admit that the new reform's, enhanced in the wake of several high-profile domestic violence scandals, were little more than a public relations ploy.

The new policy doesn't add new punishments—it enshrines the new punishments [NFL Commissioner Roger] Goodell laid out in August—but it outlines a new process for delivering them. A flow chart detailing the policy is on the NFL's web site, while ESPN has Goodell's memo to owners.

In short, the new policy establishes a process in which any player who is "formally charged with a violent crime or sexual assault" will immediately go on paid leave. Players can also be put on paid leave in the absence of charges if an independent NFL investigation "finds sufficient credible evidence that it appears a violation of the policy has occurred." Paid leave will last until the end of an NFL investigation or the conclusion of the legal process, at which point the NFL can hand down discipline. Players can then file an appeal, and the appeal process will include a hearing in front of a new expert panel that can make recommendations to Goodell. Goodell will ultimately have the authority to make the final decision on any discipline.

It's that last part that is most contentious, because aside from the NFL revising this policy without player input, it is Goodell's ultimate authority to hear appeals that the NFL Players Association opposes most. The union, which according to spokesperson George Atallah was not included in development of the new policy, wanted appeals to automatically go in front of an independent arbitrator.

And it is on that point where New England Patriots owner Robert Kraft, who was on the committee that helped design the new policy, gave away the game.

To prevent another public relations crisis, [the NFL] needed to consolidate its power and bring down even harsher punishments.

It's All About PR

The owners, Kraft said at a Wednesday press conference, considered handing that authority to an independent arbitrator. But they ultimately decided, he said, that an arbitrator was a "one-off" figure who "can compromise or water down what our best interests are." Instead, the owners left the authority with Goodell because the commissioner is "the one person who understands the long-term best interests of the game," Kraft said.

It is almost impossible, given the events of the last six months, to see that as anything but an admission that this is about public relations [PR]. That's exactly what "the best interests of the game" are.

The [Baltimore Ravens running back Ray] Rice [domestic violence] case became a PR nightmare for the NFL, largely because of the way Goodell handled it. The commissioner initially suspended Rice for two games—a lighter suspension than NFL players receive for comparably minuscule crimes—then, after public and media backlash against the league (thanks in part to the release of a video showing Rice punching his [then fiancée, now] wife, and the NFL's bungling of that too), revisited the Rice disciplinary case and suspended him indefinitely. In the midst of similar public backlash, it willy-nillyed its way to a full season suspension of Minnesota Vikings running back Adrian Peterson, who was charged with child abuse, too.

In November, after months of wrangling between Rice and the NFL, an independent arbitrator overturned the harsher second suspension. There's at least a chance that Peterson's suspension is going to get tossed too. Independent arbitration was not guaranteed in either case; in both instances, the NFLPA (NFL Player's Association) asked for independent arbitration and the NFL agreed.

A Dubious Lesson

The lesson the NFL took out of this, then, is that not that its disciplinary procedures are out of whack; that it overstepped its bounds in an attempt to mitigate public backlash to its own bungling of the Rice case; that a carefully-bargained policy with player and union input might prevent that in the future; or even that, perhaps, it shouldn't be in the business of positioning itself as our nation's moral arbiter.

The lesson it took, instead, is that to prevent another public relations crisis, it needed to consolidate its power and bring down even harsher punishments. In the best interests of the league.

To the NFL's credit, there are underlying non-disciplinary elements of the revised policy Goodell announced in August that are improvements. But the disciplinary policy itself is not meant to seriously address domestic violence and sexual assault within the league. Rather, it is about *giving off the per-*

ception that the NFL takes these incidents seriously—or at least more seriously than it took the Rice case—in order to avoid the type of months-long PR crisis it faced this fall.

(Further evidence this is a PR-driven reform: Goodell sat down with the *Wall Street Journal* to produce a puff piece about how he "blew it" during the Rice case. It was conveniently published Wednesday morning, hours before the NFL owners unanimously approved the new policy.)

In the NFL's Best Interest

It's not hard to envision what this sort of approach will lead to. As I've argued before, the absence of any player input in these decisions will virtually ensure that the disciplinary process turns into a battle over labor rights and NFL discipline. They will look a lot like what the Rice and Peterson cases have looked like so far. That isn't an accident on the NFL's part. It is a useful by-product. A negotiated process or an independent arbitrator who reins in its authority only get in the way of Goodell and the league's desire to wield the policy as a tool against players.

Which should be a reminder that Kraft wasn't being dishonest. This sort of policy is in the NFL's best interest. It positions the league, publicly anyway, to make it look as if it is taking domestic violence and sexual assault seriously, while the NFLPA and any player it represents who fight these decisions will look callous and gross by comparison (see: Adrian Peterson). That's good for the public image of the league. And, while at least part of Goodell and his owners might be sincere about taking these incidents seriously, there should be no mistake: *good for the public image of the league* is exactly what this new policy is designed to be.

The NFL Must Do More to Curb Domestic Abuse

Richard Blumenthal

Richard Blumenthal is a US senator from Connecticut. He also served five terms as that state's attorney general.

In a letter to (National Football League) NFL Commissioner Roger Goodell, U.S. Senator Richard Blumenthal (D-Conn.) today [January 30, 2015] called on the league to clarify the terms of its financial commitment to The National Domestic Violence Hotline and the National Sexual Violence Resource Center. He also called on the NFL to consider the ramifications of implementing a plan that bolsters the visibility of such groups via PSAs [public service announcements] but does not provide additional resources to the groups to handle the ensuing surge in need for services.

Blumenthal, the earliest and strongest critic of the NFL's handling of the [Baltimore Ravens running back] Ray Rice domestic violence incident [of February 2014], pressed the league's Troy Vincent at a December 2, 2014, Commerce Committee hearing on what commitments the NFL would make to help groups on the front lines of the fight against domestic violence. Although Vincent testified that the NFL was prepared to commit $5 million annually for five years to the groups, a January 15 follow-up letter from the league to Blumenthal and Sen. Brian Schatz (D-Hawaii) said some of the funding would be in the form of promotional support, raising questions about the exact nature of the commitment made and testified about before Congress. . . .

Senator Blumenthal's Letter

The full text of Blumenthal's letter to Commissioner Goodell is below:

January 30, 2015

Dear Commissioner Goodell,

While I appreciate your response of January 15, 2015, I have serious concerns about the National Football League's (NFL) real commitment to ending a culture of apparent acceptance of domestic violence and sexual assault. I welcomed the testimony from Troy Vincent at the Senate Commerce, Science and Transportation Committee hearing on December 2, 2014, in which he stated that the NFL would contribute $5 million to The National Domestic Violence Hotline (the Hotline) and the National Sexual Violence Resource Center (NSVRC) annually for the next five years.

Although I am glad the NFL has recognized the necessity of addressing this issue, this amount is barely a fraction of the financial support needed by organizations that every day provide shelter, counseling, and education across the country. Compared with the $10 million per year that is spent on its Super Bowl halftime show—not to mention the $5 billion the NFL earns each year in television rights—this amount seems terribly insufficient. If the NFL is serious about its commitment to combatting domestic violence, it could contribute many times more.

Even at the current level of commitment, when it comes to clear terms for timing and action, the NFL has hedged and dodged. The letter implies that some of the $25 million would be used for promotional support, which may include public service announcements. These supposed "public service" ads may also be self-serving—promoting the NFL's public image as much as raising awareness. Insofar as they raise public awareness, they are likely to substantially increase call volume to the Hotline as well as requests for service without actually bolstering resources for local service providers that struggle every day to help survivors rebuild their lives.

The NFL's failure to pledge resources directly to shelters and other local service providers may be seen rightly by many survivor advocates as a mockery of any real commitment. Indeed, the NFL has a special obligation to support shelters and services provided locally in the areas that have invested financially in NFL teams.

Regardless of financial commitment, the NFL so far has not articulated how it will ensure that its athletes are genuinely good role models to fans—a step that only the NFL can take towards truly shifting the culture.

Taken in totality, I believe that the NFL's handling of its response to public outcry over the league's role in domestic violence is a clear indication of why additional oversight of professional sports leagues is necessary. I plan to reintroduce the SPORTS [Sustained Promotion of Responsibility in Team Sports] Act to make sure that Congress and the public have the ability to periodically and formally review the appropriateness of the antitrust exemptions. At this time, I request a detailed timeline of how the NFL plans to meet its existing commitments and any additional measures for addressing the scourge of domestic violence and sexual assault. Thank you in advance for your cooperation with this request.

Sincerely,
Richard Blumenthal
United States Senate

Domestic Violence Is Not a Serious Problem in the NFL

Jim Picht

Jim Picht is a senior editor at Communities Digital News, *an independent, web-based community news service formerly operated by the* Washington Times.

The National Organization for Women (NOW) called for the resignation of NFL [National Football League] Commissioner Roger Goodell this week [September 2014]. They said that the NFL "has a violence against women problem."

NOW President Terry O'Neill said in a statement that "the NFL has lost its way. It doesn't have a Ray Rice problem, it has a violence against women problem." [Baltimore Ravens running back Ray Rice punched his fiancée in February 2014 and video of the incident was released in September 2014.]

Does it?

The data say no, it does not. More than that, the data say that NFL players are half as likely to commit domestic violence as men in their 20s in the general population.

A 15-year-old academic study by Alfred Blumstein and Jeff Benedict was one of the first to look at this issue. In a paper titled "Criminal Violence of NFL Players Compared to the General Population," they compared arrest data for NFL players and other men for a variety of crimes, including assault (non-domestic), domestic violence, rape, kidnapping, homicide, DUI, drugs, and property offenses.

Blumstein and Benedict found that of the 342 black players in their sample, 97 of them, or 28 percent, had an arrest for one of these crimes. There were 77 whites in the sample; seven of them, or 9 percent, had an arrest.

Those numbers appear high until we compare them with arrest numbers for the general population. The [Federal Bureau of Investigation] FBI's Uniform Crime Reports provided the arrest data. For the general population, the arrest rate for assault for black men was 6,990 per 100,00, and for whites, 2,209.

The corresponding rate for NFL players, black and white, was less than half the rate for the general population.

The NFL Arrests Database

More recently, *USA Today* published its USA Today NFL Arrests Database, which goes from 2000, just after the Blumstein-Benedict study, to today. Benjamin Morris at FiveThirtyEight's DataLab used these data with the Bureau of Crime Statistics' Arrest Data Analysis Tool to compare arrest rates for NFL players and the general population.

Feminists reject the notion of "gender symmetry" in domestic violence, but studies have found that in domestic violence cases, men strike the first blow 27 percent of the time, women 24 percent, and the violence is a mutual brawl the remainder of the time.

Morris looked only at the 25–30 age group, which most closely reflects the age of NFL players. What he found was that, again, NFL players have arrest rates far below the general population. Their arrest rates for domestic violence are half the rate of the general public, just as Blumstein and Benedict found. In addition, Morris found that NFL arrest rates for DUI [driving under the influence] were about one-fourth the general rate; for non-domestic assault, about one-sixth; for sex offenses, about one-half; and for non-violent gun-related offenses, about one-half.

Overall, arrest rates in the NFL are only 13 percent of those for the general public among men aged 25 to 30.

There are a variety of reasons for this, the most obvious being that the average income of NFL players is high, with higher arrest rates strongly correlated with lower income. It isn't possible with the existing data to sort domestic violence arrests by income level, but the fact remains: Terry O'Neill and others who claim the NFL has an unusual problem of violence against women are very wrong.

An alternative reading would be that they're correct, but that teachers, plumbers, firefighters, construction workers and college professors combined have an even bigger problem of violence against women.

Skewed Data

Another conclusion comes from the fact that about 40 percent of reported domestic violence victims are men. Researchers note that heterosexual males are much less likely to report abuse by a spouse or cohabiter to the police. Feminists reject the notion of "gender symmetry" in domestic violence, but studies have found that in domestic violence cases, men strike the first blow 27 percent of the time, women 24 percent, and the violence is a mutual brawl the remainder of the time.

If we accept these data, we are forced to conclude that women are more violent in domestic relationships than NFL players.

The video recording of Ray Rice striking his fiancée is disturbing, and a matter for police investigation (Rice was required to receive anger-management training). But the hysteria over NFL violence is just that.

What we're facing is not an epidemic of man-against-woman violence in the NFL, but of ideologically driven NFL bashing.

The current furor over NFL violence is reminiscent of another episode: In 1993, at a Pasadena news conference before that year's Super Bowl game, reporters were told by women's groups that Super Sunday was the biggest day of the year for domestic violence.

They reported that the violence rate increased by 40 percent on Super Sunday.

That "fact" was widely reported and repeated for years. It prompted public service ads to encourage men to stay calm during the game, and women to call for help before things got bad. It was obviously true; it matched what feminists believe about men and what people believe about the louts who watch football.

It was a misandrist slur. Domestic violence rates don't rise during the Super Bowl.

A "Witch Hunt"?

As a side note, we might wonder whether, like Rice, all domestic abusers, male and female, should not only be punished by the law, but by their employers and forced into unemployment. The NFL is concerned with protecting its image and has every right to fire Rice to do it, and even Goodell.

However, calls from outside the NFL to require that the NFL fire abusers would seem peculiar if aimed at journalists and professors.

Employers can fire you for any reason they please, as long as it isn't your gender, your race, your age, or your membership in any other protected class. They can certainly fire you for domestic abuse. But just how badly and how long do we think we should punish abusers, drug users, flashers and public urinators? The growing consensus seems to be, "as much as we can, and forever."

This further points to the likelihood that what we are observing is witch-hunting hysteria, not reasoned, data-driven policy.

Ray Rice is clearly the sort of man I wouldn't want dating my daughter, but he should thank his lucky stars that we no longer hang or burn witches.

The NFL Is Working Hard to Combat Domestic Violence

Lucia Graves

Lucia Graves is a staff correspondent for the National Journal, *a Washington, DC-based magazine that focuses on politics and public policy.*

After much delay, members of Congress finally have a response to recent accounts of assault and battery put forth by National Football League (NFL) players' wives—and they're not stopping with the NFL.

Sen. Jay Rockefeller, D-W.V., held a hearing on domestic violence in professional sports, broadly defined, on Tuesday afternoon [December 2, 2014], also summoning representatives from Major League Baseball, the National Basketball Association, and the National Hockey League to testify before the Senate Commerce Committee.

"Sports have always played a huge role culturally and otherwise in the United States," Sen. Rockefeller began. "Just last week on Thanksgiving, millions of Americans were probably paying more attention to their TV sets than to their turkeys." Ranking member John Thune, R-S.D., scolded the leagues for not sending their commissioners.

The hearing comes following public pressure to respond to the now-infamous video of former Baltimore Ravens running back Ray Rice knocking his then-fiancée unconscious in an elevator. The video sparked national outrage and a wave of activism, with national women's groups like UltraViolet staging elaborate campaigns to raise awareness about the issue.

Yet Rockefeller, in his opening statement was determined to broaden the scope of the conversation, noting that professional athletes of all stripes serve as role models for young Americans and ought to be held to the highest standard. "I hope we can skip protestations that domestic violence is a larger societal problem and not unique to sports," he said.

The NFL's Five-Step Plan

If protestations were what he was expecting, he didn't get any from NFL executive and former player Troy Vincent. In an emotional testimony Tuesday afternoon, Vincent said that his mother was a domestic-abuse survivor, and, in a sometimes quavering voice, he laid out five steps the NFL is taking to combat its domestic-abuse problem.

First, Vincent said, through efforts lead by the league commissioner, the NFL is conducting a "thorough review" of its conduct policy. "We will create a conduct committee responsible for review and to recommend changes to the conduct policy going forward," he said.

The league is raising awareness about domestic violence by . . . promoting programs to educate those who play, coach, and manage NFL teams about the realities of sexual assault.

Second, the league is deploying a comprehensive mandatory education program for more than 5,000 men and women associated with the NFL. What exactly the curriculum will be is less clear. "Our goal is to ensure that everyone understands and has the full scope of this behavior," Vincent said, "and is familiar with the warning signs associated with these crimes."

Third, the NFL is training critical-response teams to quickly react to family violence and sexual assault, including ensuring safety and medical, legal, and financial support. That's something NFL wives, such as Dewan Smith-Williams, have recently said the league is critically lacking. (In her account to *The Washington Post*, Smith-Williams said when she called the league to report domestic abuse, respondents would say, "'Oh, we're really sorry that you are going through this. We'll look into it.' But you never heard back. There's no one available for the wives.")

Fourth, Vincent said the league is supporting leading sexual-assault awareness and prevention groups such as the National Domestic Violence Hotline and the National Sexual Violence Resource Center, although he didn't specify what exactly that support entailed.

Fifth, the league is raising awareness about domestic violence by working in collaboration with the No More campaign and the Joyful Heart Foundation, Vincent said. This awareness will take the form of public-service announcements during games, according to Vincent's testimony, and promoting programs to educate those who play, coach, and manage NFL teams about the realities of sexual assault.

Will It Be Enough?

Such steps are unlikely to satisfy the millions of fans who felt that the NFL's response to the Ray Rice video was inadequate. Rice had been suspended indefinitely only after the video was made public, and according to league insiders, has already had several teams express interest in him. [Rice appealed the suspension and won, becoming a free agent on December 1, 2014. As of July 2015, he remains unsigned.]

A similar hearing requested by Rep. Jackie Speier, D-Calif., was pushed back indefinitely earlier this year when outgoing House Oversight and Government Reform Committee Chairman Darrell Issa, R-Calif., and ranking member Elijah Cummings, D-Md., said the hearing had been discussed but never agreed to. Now it's unclear whether it will ever go forward, as *National Journal* reported earlier this fall.

As to whether specific NFL players will be held to account for their actions? "We're working hard to balance the issues of a fair process with the goal of preventing and punishing these communities," Vincent said.

The NFL Has Strengthened Its Player-Conduct Policies

National Football League

The National Football League (NFL) is the premier league for professional American football teams.

It is a privilege to be part of the National Football League (NFL). *Everyone* who is part of the league must refrain from "conduct detrimental to the integrity of and public confidence in" the NFL. This includes owners, coaches, players, other team employees, game officials, and employees of the league office, NFL Films, NFL Network, or any other NFL business.

Conduct by anyone in the league that is illegal, violent, dangerous, or irresponsible puts innocent victims at risk, damages the reputation of others in the game, and undercuts public respect and support for the NFL. We must endeavor at all times to be people of high character; we must show respect for others inside and outside our workplace; and we must strive to conduct ourselves in ways that favorably reflect on ourselves, our teams, the communities we represent, and the NFL.

To this end, the league has increased education regarding respect and appropriate behavior, has provided resources for all employees to assist them in conforming their behavior to the standards expected of them, and has made clear that the league's goal is to prevent violations of the Personal Conduct Policy. In order to uphold our high standards, when violations of this Personal Conduct Policy do occur, appropriate disciplinary action must follow.

This Personal Conduct Policy is issued pursuant to the Commissioner's authority under the Constitution and Bylaws to address and sanction conduct detrimental to the league and professional football.

This policy applies to the Commissioner; all owners; all employees of the NFL, NFL clubs, and all NFL-related entities, including players under contract, coaches, game officials; all rookie players selected in the NFL college draft and all undrafted rookie players, unsigned veterans who were under contract in the prior League Year; and other prospective employees once they commence negotiations with a club concerning employment. Clubs and league staff are strongly encouraged to communicate this policy to independent contractors and consultants and to make clear that violations of this policy will be grounds for terminating a business relationship.

Expectations and Standards of Conduct

It is not enough simply to avoid being found guilty of a crime. We are all held to a higher standard and must conduct ourselves in a way that is responsible, promotes the values of the NFL, and is lawful.

The Commissioner may determine to place a player or other employee on leave with pay on a limited and temporary basis to permit the league to conduct an investigation.

If you are convicted of a crime or subject to a disposition of a criminal proceeding (as defined in this Policy), you are subject to discipline. But even if your conduct does not result in a criminal conviction, if the league finds that you have engaged in any of the following conduct, you will be subject to discipline. Prohibited conduct includes but is not limited to the following:

- Actual or threatened physical violence against another person, including dating violence, domestic violence, child abuse, and other forms of family violence;

- Assault and/or battery, including sexual assault or other sex offenses;

- Violent or threatening behavior toward another employee or a third party in any workplace setting;

- Stalking, harassment, or similar forms of intimidation;

- Illegal possession of a gun or other weapon (such as explosives, toxic substances, and the like), or possession of a gun or other weapon in any workplace setting;

- Illegal possession, use, or distribution of alcohol or drugs;

- Possession, use, or distribution of steroids or other performance enhancing substances;

- Crimes involving cruelty to animals as defined by state or federal law;

- Crimes of dishonesty such as blackmail, extortion, fraud, money laundering, or racketeering;

- Theft-related crimes such as burglary, robbery, or larceny;

- Disorderly conduct;

- Crimes against law enforcement, such as obstruction, resisting arrest, or harming a police officer or other law enforcement officer;

- Conduct that poses a genuine danger to the safety and well-being of another person; and

- Conduct that undermines or puts at risk the integrity of the NFL, NFL clubs, or NFL personnel. . . .

Potential Consequence

[Players] may be placed on paid administrative leave or on the Commissioner Exempt List under either of the following circumstances:

> First, you are formally charged with a crime of violence, meaning that you are accused of having used physical force or a weapon to injure or threaten another person, of having engaged in a sexual assault by force or a sexual assault of a person who was incapable of giving consent, of having engaged in other conduct that poses a genuine danger to the safety or well-being of another person, or of having engaged in animal abuse. The formal charges may be in the form of an indictment by a grand jury, the filing of charges by a prosecutor, or an arraignment in a criminal court.

> Second, if an investigation leads the Commissioner to believe that you may have violated this Policy by committing any of the conduct identified above, he may act where the circumstances and evidence warrant doing so. This decision will not reflect a finding of guilt or innocence and will not be guided by the same legal standards and considerations that would apply in a criminal trial.

Leave with Pay

In cases in which a violation relating to a crime of violence is suspected but further investigation is required, the Commissioner may determine to place a player or other employee on leave with pay on a limited and temporary basis to permit the league to conduct an investigation. Based on the results of this investigation, the player or employee may be returned to duty, be placed on leave with pay for a longer period, or be subject to discipline.

A player who is placed on the Commissioner Exempt List may not practice or attend games, but with the club's permission he may be present at the club's facility on a reasonable basis for meetings, individual workouts, therapy and rehabilitation, and other permitted non-football activities. Non-player employees placed on paid administrative leave may be present only on such basis as is approved by the Commissioner or the league disciplinary officer and only under circumstances in which they are not performing their regular duties.

A second [assault or violence] offense will result in permanent banishment from the NFL.

Leave with pay will generally last until the league makes a disciplinary decision and any appeal from that discipline is fully resolved. . . .

Discipline for Violations

Depending on the nature of the violation and the record of the employee, discipline may be a fine, a suspension for a fixed or an indefinite period of time, a requirement of community service, a combination of the three, or banishment from the league. Discipline may also include requirements to seek ongoing counseling, treatment, or therapy where appropriate as well as the imposition of enhanced supervision. It may also include a probationary period and conditions that must be met for reinstatement and to remain eligible to participate in the league. Repeat offenders will be subject to enhanced and/or expedited discipline, including banishment from the league. In determining discipline, both aggravating and mitigating factors will be considered.

Ownership and club or league management have traditionally been held to a higher standard and will be subject to more significant discipline when violations of the Personal Conduct Policy occur.

With regard to violations of the Personal Conduct Policy that involve assault, battery, domestic violence, dating violence, child abuse and other forms of family violence, or sexual assault involving physical force or committed against someone incapable of giving consent, a first offense will subject the offender to a baseline suspension without pay of six games, with consideration given to any aggravating or mitigating factors. The presence of possible aggravating factors may warrant a longer suspension. Possible aggravating factors include, but are not limited to, a prior violation of the Personal Conduct Policy, similar misconduct before joining the NFL, violence involving a weapon, choking, repeated striking, or when an act is committed against a particularly vulnerable person, such as a child, a pregnant woman, or an elderly person, or where the act is committed in the presence of a child. A second offense will result in permanent banishment from the NFL. An individual who has been banished may petition for reinstatement after one year, but there is no presumption or assurance that the petition will be granted.

Football Is a Socially Acceptable Way to Express Violent Emotions

Tom Allon

Huffington Post blogger Tom Allon is the chief executive officer and owner of City and State NY, a media company devoted solely to covering government and politics in New York. He is the former publisher of Manhattan's two largest community weeklies, Our Town *and* West Side Spirit.

Like many Americans, I have a love-hate relationship with professional football.

When it's played well and has heightened drama, like the 4th quarter of Super Bowl XLIX, there is no more thrilling spectacle than the gladiators jousting for the NFL [National Football League] crown. It is not only a game of intense physicality, with balletic twists by receivers often followed by bone-crushing hits by linebackers, but also a battle of wits and strategic warfare.

But as we were all too often reminded this year, professional football can also bring out the worst in people—with the heart-wrenching scene of domestic abuse by former Baltimore Ravens running back Ray Rice caught on camera for the world to see [2014]. When the violent culture first bred by high school and college football leads to heightened violence perpetrated by NFL players, we must take a step back and acknowledge that there is a significant downside to America's favorite spectator sport.

And it's not just inside the home (or nightclubs) where this macho and violent game leads to unnecessary harm—it's also inside the skulls of long-time players, who suffer repeated concussions and head injuries that lead to long-term brain damage. How many ex-NFL players do we have to see succumb to dementia or self-inflicted injury before we realize that there is an epidemic of brain injuries that is too high a price to pay for the mere viewing and rooting pleasure of millions of Americans?

When this football season started last fall [2014] there was a drumbeat of bad news that thundered down on the NFL: scientific studies that proved a high percentage of ex-players suffer from brain injuries followed by the Ray Rice video and the league's bungling of his punishment. I stopped watching Sunday games for a while (and since my two favorite teams, the [New York] Jets and Giants, were abysmal this helped fuel my righteous indignation).

In an era where so much of life is fragmented ... it is nice and comforting to have one night where everything is on the line and will be decided definitively.

Could Football Be in Decline?

Like some well-meaning pundits, I was ready to write football's premature obituary. To paraphrase [author] Mark Twain: "Reports of [football's] death are greatly exaggerated." I would tell friends and colleagues that watching football in 2015 reminded me of watching professional boxing in the 1980s. When that sport's most iconic figure, Muhammad Ali, started slurring his words and walking around like he was, boxing started its slow fade. Today it has been relegated to minor sport status.

Could that be the fate of professional football, I thought, a multi-billion dollar industry that would be toppled, like tobacco, because the metaphorical surgeon general's warning was finally being heeded?

It's still possible that in the not-too-distant future, football will head over the cliff and begin its slow descent. Like empires and powerful civilizations, no industry or professional sport is immune from the vagaries of excess and overreach.

But after watching Sunday night's Super Bowl, which included two star-studded teams that I have only a casual interest in, I am reminded by the powerful hold that professional football has on America's collective psyche. For one night, a large chunk of our country congregates around a big screen, all at the same time, and we watch these larger than life figures go toe-to-toe for 60 minutes in a winner-take-all death match.

Sublimating Violence

In an era where so much of life is fragmented and nuanced and exists in the gray zone, it is nice and comforting to have one night where everything is on the line and will be decided definitively. There will be a championship team, a most valuable player and a ceremony to hoist an award for one lucky team—and one lucky city (or in the case of New England, a region).

And for the next 48 hours, there is endless chatter in the Twittersphere and on Facebook and on sports radio shows picking apart the coaches decisions, analyzing the key plays and making historical comparisons to Super Bowls past. There is a unifying aspect to this collective discussion; for once, red states and blue states recede; black and white and brown and yellow fans vehemently argue for their favorite team or favorite player. The dysfunction of Congress, the sluggishness of the economy, the growing inequality in our society—it all fades into the background as people of all races and classes talk about "The Game" or "The Pass" or "That Coach's Awful Last-Minute Decision."

Professional football, the closest thing that modern society has to the Roman Coliseum, is our metaphorical civil war, our fight to the death, our gladiators fighting ferociously for the coveted gold prize. It allows millions of us to at once express and sublimate our violent and hostile emotions in a controlled and socially acceptable way.

An American Pastime

In short, football is both metaphor and the bluntest expression of American violence and rugged individualism. It is as purely American a pastime as anything that still exists; we don't see the Chinese or the Russians adopting football as their own and it's not likely that this unique game will spread globally in the same way that basketball has in recent decades. It is ours and we get to keep it all to ourselves.

But I still wish they could manufacture helmets that make concussions obsolete. Penalties for hitting players above the neck should be much more severe.

Since we're in the 21st century, maybe cheerleaders could be co-ed? And perhaps high school and college players could be required to learn feminism and gender studies so they will become less testosterone-fueled and more progesterone sympathetic.

That would be a real game changer.

CHAPTER 3

What Is the Impact of Drugs in Professional Football?

Chapter Preface

When most people think about substance abuse in the NFL, they think of the many players who have been in the news for drug and alcohol problems off the field. Headlines about professional football players arrested for driving under the influence (DUI) or getting caught with recreational drugs like marijuana or cocaine are commonplace, but the heightened media coverage of their arrests does not mean that football players as a group are more prone to using these substances than other people are.

According to data from the *USA Today* NFL Player Arrests database and the Bureau of Justice Statistics analyzed by sportswriter Benjamin Morris, NFL players are actually far less likely to be arrested for drug or alcohol offenses than men their age in the general US population.

"The most common arrests among the general public are for drug-related offenses and DUIs," writes Morris. "The most common among NFL players is DUI, with assault a distant second. Overall, NFL players' arrest rate is just 13 percent of the national average."[1] Morris's analysis further shows that the DUI rate for NFL players is just 27.5 percent of the national average, while the arrest rate for drug offenses is just 11.4 percent of the national average.

Nevertheless, players who do wind up in legal trouble over their substance use also face sanctions from the NFL in the form of fines, frequent unannounced drug testing, and suspensions that grow longer with each violation. The NFL routinely screens all players for recreational drug use at the beginning of each season, and players who fail those tests or

1. Benjamin Morris, "The Rate of Domestic Violence Arrests Among NFL Players," *Five Thirty Eight*, July 31, 2014. http://fivethirtyeight.com/datalab/the-rate-of-domestic -violence-arrests-among-nfl-players.

whose recreational drug use comes to light through legal problems are put on a program of additional testing and consequences.

But party drugs are only part of the equation when it comes to substance abuse in professional football. The use of performance-enhancing drugs (PEDs) and powerful opioid pain medications present even more formidable problems for NFL players, and for the league itself.

As professional football evolved over the past few decades to become the high-impact, adrenaline-fueled contact sport that it is today, the size, speed, and strength of its players became increasingly important. To stay competitive, many players turned to dangerous and illegal PEDs such as anabolic steroids, which increase muscle mass; amphetamines, which boost speed, focus, and reaction time; and Human Growth Hormone (HGH), which speeds injury recovery and unnaturally causes players to permanently increase their height, weight, and overall body size.

Indeed, NFL players have significantly grown in size and strength over the past fifty years, and especially over the past decade. According to data from Pro-Football-Reference.com, in the 1960s the average offensive lineman was 6-foot-3 and weighed 251 pounds. In 2011, the average was 6-foot-5 and 310 pounds. By 2014, some players weighed over 400 pounds and stood as tall as seven feet. Such a dramatic increase in height and weight cannot be explained naturally, critics say, suggesting that PEDs have likely played a significant role. Various sports commentators have opined that without PEDs—and HGH in particular—professional football would not be the game of high-performing, super-sized gladiators that it is today.

Although the NFL has strict policies about the use of PEDs and has randomly tested players for steroids for decades (both during the season and off), players are always looking for new supplements to help improve their performance, and the list of banned substances is ever-growing. Players may use some substances for years before they are banned by the league, as is the case with HGH, which some sources estimate at least 30 percent of NFL players have taken. The NFL tested players for HGH for the first time in 2014.

Besides the severe physical consequences of using PEDs—such as volatile behavior, deadly heart problems and strokes, and the disfiguring growth of hands and facial features—their use has led to another dangerous consequence; because players are bigger, stronger, and faster, they are able to hit each other much harder than did previous generations of athletes. Unsurprisingly, injuries are both now more frequent and more severe, something the NFL has tried to address by recently modifying the rules on acceptable tackling techniques and field positions.

"If players aren't freakishly huge, they won't be able to use such freakish force against their opponents," sports analyst Alexander Crowe writes in an essay that makes the case for HGH testing. The new rules mean that "we'll continue to see players give 100 percent and have great football games, just less players getting hit in the head so violently that they need a stretcher to get off the field."[2]

Performance-enhancing drugs aside, football players accept that injury is an inherent part of the game they love, and they typically endure a great deal of physical pain, both throughout their careers and long after they retire. That reality has led many current and former players to rely on powerful and addictive opioid painkillers, often first administered by team doctors or, more controversially, trainers before, during, or after games.

A 2014 lawsuit filed by retired players accuses the NFL of systematically getting them addicted to painkillers, and the re-

2. Alexander Crowe, "The Injury Crisis in the NFL; Making the Case for HGH Testing," WRST Sports, October 21, 2013. https://wrstsports.wordpress.com/2013/10/21/the-injury-crisis-in-the-nfl-making-the-case-for-hgh-testing.

cent arrest of a former Dallas Cowboys player on charges of illegally selling powerful oxycodone pain pills to undercover officers underscores the gravity of the NFL's pain-management issue. Football exacts an extreme physical toll on the body, and many players struggle with ongoing pain issues for the rest of their lives.

The authors in this chapter present a wide range of viewpoints regarding the causes and consequences of drug use in professional football, whether for pain, performance, or recreation.

NFL Players Routinely Abuse Pain Medications to Stay in the Game

John Barr

John Barr is a reporter in ESPN's enterprise unit.

Kyle Turley remembers the plane rides home when he first came into the NFL [National Football League], those hours spent folding his 6-foot-5 frame into an airline seat after a Sunday afternoon full of violent collisions with other 300-pound men.

An offensive lineman for eight years with the Saints, Rams and Chiefs who retired after the 2007 season, Turley said it was commonplace to find comfort in the form of two Miller Lites. But the real relief, Turley said, would come when members of the Saints' medical staff routinely handed out the prescription painkiller Vicodin on the flights home.

"The trainers and the doctors used to go down the aisle and say, 'Who needs what?'" Turley said. "If you had something hurting and needed a painkiller to take the edge off so you could sleep that night, they made sure you had it."

A scientific study conducted by researchers at Washington University in St. Louis found that retired NFL players misuse opioid pain medications at a rate more than four times that of the general population. The study, co-funded by ESPN and the National Institute on Drug Abuse, provides new evidence to suggest the roots of that misuse can be traced to the misuse of painkillers during players' NFL careers. The research findings were published Jan. 28, [2011] in *Drug and Alcohol Dependence*, a peer-reviewed, scientific journal.

When asked about their prescription painkiller use while playing in the NFL, 52 percent of the retired players surveyed said they used prescription pain medication. Of those users, 71 percent admitted misusing the drugs during their playing days and, of that same group, 63 percent said they obtained the pills from a nonmedical source: a teammate, coach, trainer, family member, dealer or the Internet.

Under pressure to perform on Sundays ... players routinely numb their NFL injuries with prescription painkillers and risk long-term debilitating injuries.

"It tells me that there has to be more evaluation, more monitoring," said Linda Cottler, a professor of epidemiology in Washington University's Department of Psychiatry, who directed the research. "That's a problem, I think, that only 37 percent got [prescription pain medications] exclusively from a doctor."

The Legal Risks of Fighting NFL Pain

Turley, who now leads a country- and rock-infused band, said pain medication was new to him when he arrived in the NFL.

"I never took a Vicodin in college, ever," he said. "I didn't even know what Vicodin was until I got to the NFL."

Under pressure to perform on Sundays, Turley said, players routinely numb their NFL injuries with prescription painkillers and risk long-term debilitating injuries.

"I know guys that have bought thousands of pills," Turley said. "Tons of guys would take Vicodin before a game."

Turley said one physician outside the NFL's network of doctors—he would not identify the individual by name—once offered to sell him a bag of 10,000 Vicodin. The going rate, Turley recalled, was $3 per pill. He said he didn't make the purchase.

"Everybody has a guy," Turley said.

The NFL has had a few high-profile cases involving pain-killers.

In April 2008, New England Patriots offensive tackle Nick Kaczur was pulled over for speeding in Whitestown, N.Y., while driving back to his home in Massachusetts.

The officer noted in a police report that Kaczur appeared "extremely nervous." The officer said he found a "Ziploc bag-gie" in the center console, containing four pills, later discovered to be the prescription painkiller Percocet. When he continued searching, the officer found another "Ziploc baggie" in Kaczur's sweatshirt pocket containing 202 OxyContin pills, according to the report.

Kaczur was cited for criminal possession of a controlled substance and speeding. According to court documents, Kaczur told police he'd obtained the pills from a man named "Danny," whom he met at a Boston-area bar months earlier.

At that time, Kaczur was coming off a career year. He'd started 15 games at right tackle the previous season and was part of a Patriots offensive line that allowed just 21 sacks, the fewest for the franchise in 30 years.

The Oxycodone Connection

Faced with an embarrassing criminal case involving illegally obtained prescription painkillers, Kaczur cut a deal, offering to wear a recording device to help investigators from the Drug Enforcement Administration [DEA] arrest his dealer, "Danny," in exchange for a lighter penalty.

"Danny" was Daniel Ekasala. According to a DEA report, Kaczur met Ekasala in November 2007. For nearly six months, according to court documents, Kaczur purchased "approximately one hundred 80mg OxyContin pills every three or four days from [Ekasala]." In a sentencing memorandum he filed as part of the federal court case, Ekasala's Boston-based attorney, Bernard Grossberg, wrote:

"The Confidential Source [Kaczur] befriended the defendant [Ekasala] and implored him to furnish Oxycodone with the explanation that it was widely used in the NFL and that players, especially interior linemen, needed the painkillers in order to endure the injuries they suffered and in order to continue to play."

In March 2009, former Philadelphia Eagles defensive tackle Sam Rayburn sent two men into separate pharmacies in his hometown of Chickasha, Okla., with prescriptions Rayburn had stolen from a doctor's office and forged.

Kaczur, who finished this past NFL season on injured reserve due to a back injury, declined to comment to ESPN, as did the Patriots.

Ekasala, who pleaded guilty and was sentenced to 42 months in prison, declined to comment to ESPN for this report when reached at the Federal Correctional Institution in Fort Dix, N.J.

Pharmacy Fraud

In March 2009, former Philadelphia Eagles defensive tackle Sam Rayburn sent two men into separate pharmacies in his hometown of Chickasha, Okla., with prescriptions Rayburn had stolen from a doctor's office and forged. When a suspicious pharmacist called police, Rayburn was arrested on two counts of attempting to obtain a controlled substance by forgery or fraud. He faced 20 years in prison if convicted.

Rayburn, who pleaded guilty, spoke in detail to "Outside the Lines" about his painkiller addiction, which he said stemmed from NFL-related injuries and at its peak involved consuming more than 100 Percocet pills a day. He avoided prison time by going to court-ordered drug counseling and by submitting to 18 months of drug tests.

"I think if I would have given it another two or three months, it probably would have killed me," Rayburn said of his addiction. "I don't have any doubts whatsoever that it would have turned into a death situation, because I didn't see any way of slowing down."

Last May, former San Diego Chargers safety Kevin Ellison was arrested by Redondo Beach, Calif., police and charged with one count of possession of a controlled substance. Police say Ellison was found in his car in the middle of the afternoon with 100 Vicodin, which he allegedly obtained without a prescription. He was released on a $10,000 bond and has since pleaded not guilty. His case is pending.

Ellison and his agent, Jerome Stanley, both declined to comment to ESPN, but Stanley did tell *The San Diego Union-Tribune* that Ellison "thought it was a good idea to get enough pain killers to last the season. They were for him to use because of his knee surgery."

In a prepared statement, the Chargers said no one on the team's medical staff ever provided Vicodin to Ellison.

We made a determination in the late '80s that all prescription medications would be locked away in a locked cabinet.

The Painkiller Revolving Door Is Closing

In his 1994 book, *You're Okay, It's Just a Bruise,* former Oakland Raiders team doctor Robert Huizenga describes the freewheeling approach to medical care within NFL locker rooms and the lax controls that often existed for prescription painkillers. Hired in 1983, when he was fresh out of Harvard Medical School, Huizenga described his first visit to the Raiders' medical treatment room:

"On the back wall were slide-out shelves filled with aspirin-like medications, antibiotics, and cold pills. A large brown safe was pushed against the back corner. It housed potentially addictive prescription medications: bottles of Cheracol-X with codeine cough medicine, sleepers and codeine pain pills. The safe door was wide open."

"It used to be that every shop ran itself kind of like a McDonald's franchise, and league policy had nothing to do with medical care," Dr. Pierce Scranton, a team doctor for the Seattle Seahawks for 18 years, told ESPN. Scranton also served as a president of the NFL Physicians Society.

Scranton, who likened NFL medical care in the 1980s to the "Wild West," said he made a conscious decision to be more cautious with prescription painkillers.

"We made a determination in the late '80s that all prescription medications would be locked away in a locked cabinet," he said. Scranton acknowledged that he was motivated not only by medical ethics but also self-interest.

"No way was I going to go to court because a guy's kidneys shut down because a trainer dispensed medication without my knowledge," Scranton said.

A Discernable Shift

From 1998, the time he entered the NFL, to 2007, the time of his retirement, Turley said he noticed a discernible shift within the walls of NFL facilities with regard to the way prescription painkillers were stored and handed out to players. Prescription painkillers with names like Vicodin, Percocet and OxyContin became more difficult to get from team doctors and trainers.

"My last two years in Kansas City weren't the same. You didn't get it as easily," Turley said.

Baltimore Ravens center Matt Birk, a veteran of 13 NFL seasons, has witnessed a similar evolution in the drug culture inside and outside of the NFL bubble.

"I've played with a few players that have acquired pain meds on their own, through other avenues other than a team doctor," Birk said. "I've known guys who felt like they needed to obtain those medications in order to play."

Those players, Birk said, were all either offensive or defensive linemen. He said the players got the drugs from outside doctors or drug dealers.

In Birk's experience, which includes a decade with the Minnesota Vikings, team doctors were responsible in the way they stored and dispensed prescription painkillers.

"They're pretty cautious. They're not just passing them out," Birk said. "I could count on one hand the times I was given one painkiller. I've never been prescribed a bottle of 30 of them or anything like that."

"Common Stock" Medications

The prescription pain medications stored at team facilities— referred to within league medical circles as "common stock"— are required to be kept under lock and key in secure rooms. Team medical staffs are subject to routine pill-by-pill audits conducted by league security officials, all designed to ensure the medications are stored and prescribed responsibly.

Even with the league-mandated controls on painkillers, there are recent examples of alleged security breaches.

"We as physicians do our best to do the right thing and really be clean," said Dr. Patrick Connor, president of the NFL Physicians Society and team doctor for the Carolina Panthers.

Connor said he was unaware of any players going outside of team doctors to obtain prescription pain medications in order to cope with NFL injuries.

"Players often play hurt," he said. "But no, I don't think that I would take that fact and then jump to the conclusion that there's a pain medication problem."

Even with the league-mandated controls on painkillers, there are recent examples of alleged security breaches.

Coaching Staff Is Also Suspect

In April 2010 Geoffrey Santini, a 31-year veteran of the FBI who worked as director of security for the New Orleans Saints, sued his former NFL employer. Santini accused Saints general manager Mickey Loomis of ordering a cover-up after Santini revealed to Loomis that a member of the Saints' coaching staff was caught on a security camera stealing Vicodin out of the team's drug locker.

That same Saints staffer allegedly used some of the 130 stolen pills and provided the rest to another member of the coaching staff, according to Santini's lawsuit. Rather than engage in an alleged cover-up of stolen painkillers, Santini said he quit and sued the Saints for lost wages.

According to several ... warrants, Dr. David Chao, an orthopedic surgeon who serves as a [San Diego] Chargers team doctor, allegedly wrote 108 prescriptions with himself listed as the patient, an apparent violation of federal drug laws.

While Santini never named names in his lawsuit, he told some media outlets that assistant head coach Joe Vitt was the person allegedly caught on tape stealing the Vicodin pills, and head coach Sean Payton allegedly received some of those pills. Santini withdrew his lawsuit against the club in May; the claims are being handled in arbitration.

He and his attorney, Donald Hyatt II, both declined to comment to ESPN for this story.

Greg Bensel, the Saints' vice president of communications, released a prepared statement about the lawsuit.

"A former employee who resigned just before the 2009 regular season threatened to go public with these unfounded charges unless we agreed to pay him an exorbitant sum of money," Bensel said. "We refused, and now he has gone public. We will aggressively defend these false allegations in court."

In a prepared statement, Payton said: "I have reviewed Geoff Santini's lawsuit and the unwarranted publicity it has received. . . . I have never abused or stolen Vicodin or any other medication, and I fully support the Saints' position in this matter."

The DEA's Shifting Focus

According to federal court documents obtained by ESPN, Santini's lawsuit, combined with the arrest of the former Chargers safety Ellison for possession of Vicodin just a month later, prompted action from the federal Drug Enforcement Administration.

In June, DEA agents in San Diego filed a series of administrative inspection warrants and searched the medical facilities of both the San Diego Chargers and San Diego Padres, along with several of the pharmacies that provided medications to the teams.

According to several of those warrants, Dr. David Chao, an orthopedic surgeon who serves as a Chargers team doctor, allegedly wrote 108 prescriptions with himself listed as the patient, an apparent violation of federal drug laws.

RSF Pharmaceuticals, one of the pharmacies involved in the DEA searches, issued a statement saying Chao "did not write prescriptions for himself" and the medications "were for use by the Chargers medical staff to treat players."

Chao was never accused of abusing the medications, and no criminal charges were filed. The case is pending, according to the DEA. The Chargers declined to comment to ESPN, as did Chao, when reached through his attorney.

But the Chargers example helped clarify the legal gray area NFL team physicians frequently find themselves in when faced with athletes in pain.

Prepared for Pain

According to a DEA spokesperson, it is commonplace for NFL team doctors to acquire and store large quantities of prescription painkillers with no patient in mind—the idea being that team doctors are then prepared when players are injured, in pain and in need of relief. The practice is legal.

But ESPN learned that in August, DEA officials, mindful of the civil lawsuit in New Orleans and the developing situation in San Diego, hosted a meeting in Washington, D.C., which was attended by representatives of the NFL, including Dr. Connor of the NFL Physicians Society.

Connor told ESPN the purpose of the meeting was so DEA officials could make certain NFL team physicians fully understood the federal laws governing the storage and safe handling of prescription pain medications.

"There's no question that the DEA is paying closer attention," Connor said. "The pendulum has shifted over to prescription pain medication, just as it was on the performance-enhancing drug issues in the past."

One area of concern for the DEA, Connor said, was the way in which painkillers were routinely given to players on NFL road trips.

According to several current and former NFL players who spoke to ESPN, it was commonplace for team doctors and trainers to hand out pain pills after away games.

Only a DEA registrant, a team physician, can dispense prescription pain medication. Team trainers should never hand out the drugs.

Turley's memories of Vicodin being passed out on the team plane during his time with the Saints serve as a typical example.

"You can't do that. It's got to be somebody that's licensed to distribute within the state," said Rusty Payne, a DEA spokesman.

Trainers Are in a Difficult Position

Payne said that only a DEA registrant, a team physician, can dispense prescription pain medication. Team trainers should never hand out the drugs, Payne said.

"The trainers are in a bad position," Turley said. "They are participants in a corrupt system. They are taking orders from team doctors and coaches. They are told to do whatever it takes to keep players on the field."

Leamor Kahanov, a professor at Indiana State University's Department of Applied Medicine and Rehabilitation and a certified athletic trainer, helped write the prescription drug protocols used by the National Athletic Trainers' Association, the governing body for NFL trainers.

When told of the accounts of Turley and other players, Kahanov, who has not worked in the NFL, said: "We can't dispense medication. We have no prescriptive authority."

When asked specifically about Turley's account of Saints trainers handing out pain pills on the team plane, Kahanov said: "Whether those claims are true would need to be investigated."

Connor said NFL team physicians have recently taken steps to ensure they're in compliance with DEA regulations. Team doctors in host cities, for example, have now made provisions to make some of their "common stock" prescription painkillers available to visiting teams, Connor said, removing the need for a visiting team physician to prescribe drugs outside the area permitted by the state license.

"The expectation of the DEA is that people follow the rules. But I suppose . . . the expectation is that everybody will drive 65 mph and not everybody does," Connor said.

A Different Road to the Super Bowl

Back in Nashville, Turley is busy pursuing his new career, which will lead him to this year's Super Bowl. He's in the midst of a music tour that will end in Dallas next week.

For Turley, now 35, the long days and nights spent on the road take their toll. For the past few years he's dealt with post-concussion symptoms, which he links to his NFL career, and frightening episodes of vertigo. Prescription painkillers remain a part of his life.

"I still get painkillers from a source that I have. Some days are worse than others," Turley said. "I've got a little stash of my own painkillers and muscle relaxers. I didn't get them from a doctor."

Turley is also a staunch proponent of legalizing marijuana for medical reasons and said he frequently smokes marijuana to relieve NFL-related pain.

Turley remains angry about the quality of medical care he received while in the NFL. When asked for possible solutions that might reduce the degree to which players rely on pain medications, Turley stressed the need for guaranteed contracts, so players won't feel such intense pressure to play injured.

"The majority of players walk away beaten and tattered," Turley said. "The reality is, it's a violent game, and the violent outcome is pain."

Retired NFL Players Bear Serious Consequences from Drug Use

Jim Dryden

Jim Dryden is the director of broadcasts and podcasts at Washington University in St. Louis, where the study discussed in this viewpoint was conducted. The research itself was commissioned and supported by a grant from ESPN, with additional funding from the National Institute on Drug Abuse of the National Institutes of Health.

Retired NFL [National Football League] players use painkillers at a much higher rate than the rest of us, according to new research conducted by investigators at Washington University School of Medicine in St. Louis.

The researchers say the brutal collisions and bone-jarring injuries associated with football often cause long-term pain, which contributes to continued use and abuse of painkilling medications.

The study is published online in the journal *Drug and Alcohol Dependence*. It involved 644 former NFL players who retired from football between 1979 and 2006. Researchers asked them about their overall health, level of pain, history of injuries, concussions and use of prescription pain pills.

The study found that 7 percent of the former players were currently using painkilling opioid drugs. That's more than four times the rate of opioid use in the general population. Opioids are commonly prescribed for their analgesic, or pain-relieving, properties. Medications that fall within this class of drugs include morphine, Vicodin, codeine and oxycodone.

"We asked about medications they used during their playing careers and whether they used the drugs as prescribed or whether they had ever taken them in a different way or for different reasons," says principal investigator Linda B. Cottler, PhD, professor of epidemiology in psychiatry at Washington University. "More than half used opioids during their NFL careers, and 71 percent had misused the drugs. That is, they had used the medication for a different reason or in a different way than it was prescribed, or taken painkillers that were prescribed for someone else."

Among the men who currently use prescription opioids, whether misused or not, 75 percent said they had severe pain, and about 70 percent reported moderate-to-severe physical impairment.

Those who misused the drugs during their playing days were more likely to continue misusing them after retiring from football. Some 15 percent of those who misused the drugs as active players still were misusing them in retirement. Only 5 percent of former players who took the drugs as prescribed misused them after they retired from the NFL.

Living in Pain

Cottler, director of the Epidemiology and Prevention Research Group in the Department of Psychiatry, says it's not clear from the study whether retired players became dependent on the drugs. What is clear from the survey, she says, is that retired NFL players continue to live with a lot of pain.

"The rate of current, severe pain is staggering," she says. "Among the men who currently use prescription opioids, whether misused or not, 75 percent said they had severe pain, and about 70 percent reported moderate-to-severe physical impairment."

Pain was one of the main predictors of current misuse. Another was undiagnosed concussion. Retired NFL players in the study experienced an average of nine concussions each. Some 49 percent had been diagnosed with a concussion at some point during their playing careers, but 81 percent suspected they had concussions that were not diagnosed. Some players believed they may have had up to 200 concussions during their playing days.

"Many of these players explained that they didn't want to see a physician about their concussions at the time," says Simone M. Cummings, PhD, a senior scientist in psychiatry who conducted phone interviews with the former players. "These men said they knew if they reported a concussion, they might not be allowed to play. And if you get taken out of a game too many times, you can lose your spot and get cut from the team."

Self-Medicating

She says players with suspected-but-undiagnosed concussions reported they borrowed pills from teammates, friends or relatives to treat the pain themselves, thus misusing opioids in an attempt to remain in the NFL. Although 37 percent of the retired players reported that they had received opioids only from a doctor, the other 63 percent who took the drugs during their NFL careers admitted that on occasion they got the medication from someone other than a physician.

Retired players currently misusing opioid drugs also are more likely to be heavy drinkers, according to Cottler.

"So these men are at elevated risk for potential overdose," she says. "They reported more than 14 drinks a week, and many were consuming at least 20 drinks per week, or the equivalent of about a fifth of liquor."

The ESPN sports television network commissioned the study, which also was funded by the National Institute on Drug Abuse. The ESPN program "Outside the Lines" spoke informally to many retired players about their use of painkillers. One reported taking up to 1,000 Vicodin tablets per month. Another reported ingesting 100 pills per day and spending more than $1,000 per week on painkillers.

Former St. Louis Rams offensive lineman Kyle Turley said in a statement to ESPN that he knew of many players who took drugs to help them deal with the pain inflicted by the injuries they sustained in the NFL.

The offensive linemen were twice as likely as other players to use or misuse prescription pain medicines during their NFL careers.

"I know guys that have bought thousands of pills," Turley said. "Tons of guys would take Vicodin before a game."

The researchers say offensive linemen had particularly high rates of use and misuse of opioids.

"The offensive linemen were twice as likely as other players to use or misuse prescription pain medicines during their NFL careers," Cottler says. "In addition, this group tends to be overweight and have cardiovascular problems, so they represent a group of former players whose health probably should be monitored closely."

More Follow-up Is Needed

In fact, Cottler says it would be a good idea to continue monitoring everyone who has played in the NFL. She says this study revealed that some 47 percent of retired players reported having three or more serious injuries during their NFL careers, and 61 percent said they had knee injuries. Over half, 55 percent, reported that an injury ended their careers.

"These are elite athletes who were in great physical condition when their playing careers began," she says. "At the start of their careers, 88 percent of these men said they were in excellent health. By the time they retired, that number had fallen to 18 percent, primarily due to injuries. And after retirement, their health continued to decline. Only 13 percent reported that they currently are in excellent health. They are dealing with a lot of injuries and subsequent pain from their playing days. That's why they continue to use and misuse pain medicines."

Alcohol and Drug Use by NFL Players Sets a Bad Example for Youth

Bryan Levy

Bryan Levy is a writer at the Guardian Liberty Voice, *a newspaper in Las Vegas, Nevada.*

In a quiet time during the NFL [National Football League] offseason, the only news making the scene these days is the plague of substance abuse. On July 5, [2014] Cleveland Browns wide receiver Josh Gordon was arrested for driving while impaired. A few days earlier, on July 3, Indianapolis Colts wide receiver LaVon Brazill was suspended for one year for violating the league's substance abuse policy after failing a drug test. Adding to the problems is Johnny Manziel, a newly drafted quarterback for the Browns, who was photographed in a Las Vegas bathroom rolling up a $20 bill.

On July 3, reports began surfacing saying that LaVon Brazill, a 25-year-old wide receiver for the Indianapolis Colts, had failed a drug test. This is not the first time Brazill has had a run in with drugs. After being drafted by the Colts in 2012, Brazill was suspended by the team for the initial four games of the 2013 season. At the time, Brazill said that he had learned his lesson, and would choose money over weed. Two seasons later, and he is out for the year without pay. When Brazill does manage to make it onto the field for the Colts, he has shown himself to be a promising asset, with 23 catches and three touchdowns in 25 games.

The Cleveland Browns are having their own problems. WR Josh Gordon was detained in Raleigh, North Carolina on the night of July 5 driving a car that was not his while he was drunk. The official charge is that Gordon was driving while impaired, not intoxicated. Gordon was driving a car that belonged to PJ Hairston, a guard for the Charlotte Hornets. Gordon's blood alcohol level was reported as being .09. When reporters asked if there were drugs involved with the arrest, police spokespeople said they could not comment on the matter, but that there were no charges pending concerning drugs. Like Brazill, this is not Josh Gordon's first run in with substance abuse. Last season, he was suspended for two games for violating the policy. Only recently Gordon failed a drug test which put him up for a year suspension from the NFL.

The NFL finds itself plagued with substance abuse problems, and these three rising stars are part of it.

Athletes as Role Models

Finally, there is Johnny Manziel, also known as Johnny Football. Manziel played his college career at Texas A&M, where he was no stranger to controversy off the field. He was arrested in 2012, before becoming A&M's starting quarterback. In the summer of 2013, the NCAA investigated reports as to whether or not Manziel violated his amateur status after being paid for autographs. While the NCAA did not find any evidence of Manziel accepting cash, he was suspended for the first half of their season opener. Now, as Manziel prepares for his first season after being drafted by the Cleveland Browns, he continues to make headlines for his off the field behavior. First, there was a picture of him partying with teen heartthrob and troublemaker Justin Bieber, and this week a photo surfaced of Manziel in a Las Vegas bathroom, rolling up a $20 bill, like one does when snorting cocaine. While there is no visible cocaine in the picture, and some analysts say that he could just be tweaking the media, it is still not a good look for a young man who has been criticized for his behavior when not playing ball.

The Party Life Versus a Successful Career

The NFL finds itself plagued with substance abuse problems, and these three rising stars are part of it. LaVon Brazill and Josh Gordon are two young men with a serious problem, and Johnny Manziel feels that problem is something to make fun of. Perhaps he truly was just goosing the media, creating a story where there was none. In a culture where our sports stars are, like it or not, role models, it is an inappropriate joke to make, especially when the NFL is struggling with athletes who continually engage in foolish behavior. Manziel, Gordon, and Brazill need to take stock of their lives and careers. They need to decide which is more important: the party lifestyle, or the money that could be made from a successful career as a professional athlete. LaVon Brazill and possibly Josh Gordon will have a year to think about this. Hopefully, Johnny Manziel will not need that kind of time.

Pain and Pain Management in NFL Spawn a Culture of Prescription Drug Use and Abuse

Sally Jenkins and Rick Maese

Sally Jenkins and Rick Maese write for The Washington Post.

When Fred Smoot, a former Washington Redskins defensive back, fractured his sternum and had to spend four months sleeping in a recliner because he couldn't lie flat, he said his team doctors gave him a choice: Miss the rest of the season or "figure out a way to play." Worried about his livelihood, he made it on the football field each Sunday thanks to a syringe full of a drug called Toradol.

"Painkillers are like popping aspirin," Smoot said. "They get to that point."

When the throbbing in his surgically repaired right knee made it hard to walk, much less play, Chester Pitts, a former offensive lineman for the Houston Texans, found a way to prolong his career one more year: a cocktail of Toradol injections on Sundays, with anti-inflammatories and narcotic painkillers the other days of the week.

"If I was really hurting, I would take a mix," he said. "I could do Tylenol with the Indocin or the Vicodin. Couldn't do Vicodin with certain things. You could take one NSAID and one acetaminophen, whatever they said."

When former Redskin Mark Schlereth, a veteran of 12 seasons and 29 surgeries, underwent a kidney-stone operation on a Sunday night and suited up for a game less than 24 hours later, he drew the strength to do so from a needle and pill bottle.

"I would strap a dog turd to it if I thought that would make me feel better," he said. "Bottom line is, I'd do whatever I have to do. Have I had Toradol shots? Yes. Have I abused anti-inflammatories? Yes. Have I used painkillers? Yes. Have I got shot up with painkillers and Xylocaine and different things to numb areas so I can play? Yes. I've done it all."

Jarring hits and injuries are an inherent part of the National Football League, and so too is the game's complex—and potentially dangerous—system of managing pain. It's an issue the league has grappled with for many years: a culture of prescription drug use and misuse that stretches from the locker room into retirement, and even on to coaching staffs, with uneven oversight and a lack of uniform guidelines. Numerous studies suggest the drugs that help many athletes take the field each Sunday can carry dangerous side effects, lead to lifelong addictions, expose them to further injury and compromise a delicate system that's ripe for abuse.

The league's widespread use of Toradol, in particular, offers a window on the game's reliance on pills and needles.

Court records and interviews reveal that until recently some NFL teams either flouted or were ignorant of Drug Enforcement Agency laws governing the dispensing of painkillers. Moreover, *The Washington Post* surveyed more than 500 former players about their experiences with drugs in the NFL. One in four said he felt pressure from team doctors to take medication he was uncomfortable with.

The NFL's most recently reported rate of opioid use—7 percent—was three times higher than that of the general population, but the league's defenders say that the NFL's problem with prescription abuse is hardly unique. According to federal statistics, more than 2 million Americans are addicted to painkillers. Deaths caused by the overdose of prescription drugs exceeded motor vehicle deaths in 2009, according to the Centers for Disease Control and Prevention, and are responsible for more deaths than illegal street drugs, such as cocaine, heroin and amphetamines.

"The whole issue of pain meds is a big, important issue in our society well outside the NFL," said Jeff Pash, the NFL's executive vice president. "It's something that needs to be addressed on a broad basis, not just in NFL, and it is something our doctors are looking at."

The league's widespread use of Toradol, in particular, offers a window on the game's reliance on pills and needles. In *The Post* survey of retired players, 50 percent of those who retired in the 1990s or later reported using the controversial painkiller during their careers; roughly seven out of 10 who left the game in 2000 or later said they used the drug.

A 2000 survey of NFL physicians found that 28 of 30 teams used Toradol injections on game days. Another study two years later found an average of 15 pregame injections per team. Players describe pregame lines of as many as two dozen players deep waiting for a shot or a pill. "No doubt about it, I was in that line," Hall of Famer Warren Sapp said. "They're like Tic Tacs. You walked in, you got it and you played the game."

Despite warnings and mounting concerns, Toradol and a variety of other pain medications were used regularly last season, team physicians say.

Toradol is a nonsteroidal anti-inflammatory drug—not a narcotic—and though it's not addictive, it's available only with a prescription. It's often used to manage post-operative pain, and the drug is considered dangerous enough that some European countries have banned it, while others administer it only in hospitals. Among the potential side effects of overuse are kidney damage and gastrointestinal bleeding. In the case of NFL players it can be particularly problematic because it deadens feeling, inhibiting an athlete's ability to feel pain and sense injury.

Physicians say the potential for side effects is heightened by the overuse of Toradol or the "stacking" of multiple drugs. Several players interviewed for this story said they typically used Toradol in combination with other nonsteroidal anti-inflammatory drugs, or NSAIDs, over the course of a week.

Perhaps worst of all, because it is an anticoagulant, many fear it could exacerbate the effects of concussions. On that basis, as part of the massive concussion litigation brought by ex-players that the league is fighting in U.S. District Court, 11 former players have filed a lawsuit claiming their team doctors repeatedly treated them with Toradol without properly advising them of the dangers.

Despite warnings and mounting concerns, Toradol and a variety of other pain medications were used regularly last season, team physicians say. Andrew Brandt, who spent nearly a decade in the Green Bay Packers' front office, likened it to armor.

"It's part of their game-day routine," said Brandt, who now works as an analyst for ESPN. "Just like getting taped."

Pain Leads to Abuse

When linebacker Scott Fujita, a 10-year veteran free agent who has played for the Kansas City Chiefs, New Orleans Saints and Cleveland Browns, was in his prime, he used prescription drugs four to five days a week in order to play. He estimates this put him on the low end of usage among his teammates.

On Thursdays, Fridays and Saturdays, Fujita might rely on Celebrex or another anti-inflammatory. If the pain from a specific injury was really bad, the linebacker might turn to Vicodin or Percocet. On Sundays, he'd get a Toradol shot before taking the field. Then with fresh aches and pains, he'd spend Mondays on another pill to help recovery. Tuesdays and Wednesdays, though, were always different—"your chance to detox a bit."

"We called it DFW," he said. "Drug-Free Wednesday."

Fujita says he has suffered dozens of injuries during his career, from cuts requiring stitches to broken fingers to separated shoulders and torn muscles. To manage the constant pain, he has used "everything under the sun."

Pain is the inescapable price of an NFL career, and a drug problem can easily become one, too. Retired NFL players misuse opioids at a rate more than four times that of their peers, according to a 2010 study of 644 league veterans by the Washington University School of Medicine in St. Louis. Even upon retirement, 15 percent of those who misused opioids during their careers continued to misuse, according to the study, even though they were no longer playing.

"People spend so much time talking about HGH, steroids, and I think these are the real performance enhancers," Fujita said.

In a sport with short career spans and few guaranteed contracts, playing through pain is an understood job requirement.

NFL doctors say they face a constant challenge in identifying players who legitimately need prescription painkillers, as opposed to those who want pain relief without a documentable injury. Anthony Casolaro, the Redskins' team physician, said before he administers any pregame medication, he makes sure the player appeared on the week's injury report and received treatment for a specific ailment.

But the Washington University School of Medicine study reflected the prevalence of prescription drug use and abuse in the league: 52 percent of respondents said they used opioids during their career. Of those, 71 percent reported "misuse" of them.

"Part of playing in the NFL is dealing with pain. People get hurt, people take painkillers, that's just part of the game," said Frank Mattiace, a former NFL player who's now an addiction counselor and the executive director of the New Jersey-based New Pathway Counseling Services. "So you're dealing with a double-edged sword. It's such an ingrained part of their mentality."

In a sport with short career spans and few guaranteed contracts, playing through pain is an understood job requirement. In *The Post*'s survey of former players, nearly nine in 10 reported playing games while hurt. Fifty-six percent said they did this "frequently." Almost half of those who played through pain (49 percent) said they wished they had done so "less often," and an overwhelming number—68 percent—said they did not feel like they had a choice as to whether to play hurt.

With pain management such a constant challenge in NFL training rooms, football teams buy drugs in bulk. William Barr, the director of neuropsychology at the New York University School of Medicine, served as a concussion consultant for the New York Jets from 1995 to 2004. He recalls experiencing a headache and requesting aspirin from team trainers.

"They said, 'Go over there and it will deal with your headache,'?" Barr said. "There was a huge candy jar of Toradol."

Rampant Use of Toradol

The Food and Drug Administration in 1989 approved a new NSAID called ketorolac, which hit the market as Toradol. The FDA now lists more than 25 makers of it.

Toradol's fast-acting properties can be alluring in a business where job security is directly tied to health and a player's ability to perform. An intramuscular injection can have onset within 10 minutes, peaking within an hour and showing a half-life of 6 1/2 hours, according to studies.

"Once you get your first one, you realize, wow, you can play pretty pain-free for the entire game," said Tyoka Jackson, a former defensive end who played in the NFL from 1994 to 2006. "So whatever's ailing you, you don't feel."

A spokesman for Roche, which was first to put the drug on the market, declined to discuss the drug's use in football, instead referring to the FDA's recommendations. "It should be used for the short-term treatment of moderate to severe pain in adults," Chris Vancheri, the spokesman, said in an e-mail. "It is usually used before or after medical procedures or after surgery."

While the drug's potency and possible side effects worry some physicians, it's the misuse of Toradol that's particularly worrisome to doctors such as Victor Ibrahim, a team physician for D.C. United, who is also director of the Performance and Musculoskeletal Regeneration Center in Washington.

Because of its blood-thinning properties, Toradol use could have aggravated the effects of concussions suffered during their playing careers.

In *The Post*'s survey of ex-players, nearly eight in 10 of past Toradol users said they took the drug as a masking agent, intended to dull the pain they expected to feel during games. "When you mask pain and give a patient a false sense of a cure, you potentially expose them to further harm," Ibrahim said.

Joe Horn, a wide receiver who played in the NFL from 1996 to 2007, said toward the end of his career he used Toradol most every Sunday, sometimes "just in case I got injured. In case something happened, I could still make it through the game."

Team physicians, he said, never discussed with him possible side effects, which serves as a central complaint in a lawsuit that Horn and 10 other former players have filed against the NFL. The plaintiffs say that because of its blood-thinning properties, Toradol use could have aggravated the effects of concussions suffered during their playing careers.

Several physicians, though, said further studies and research are needed to understand the extent of any such dangers.

"I think that's a theoretical risk," said neurologist Michael Yochelson, the medical director for MedStar National Rehabilitation Hospital, "particularly if you're taking it beyond the recommended frequency that it might put you at a slightly increased risk for a bleed if you were to have a significant head impact."

The league has become increasingly sensitive to issues surrounding the drug, to the point that last season some NFL physicians attempted to get players to sign Toradol releases protecting them from liability "for any injury, damage or death sustained" from using it. The NFL Players Association filed a grievance against the league and NFL management council in December, demanding the waivers be nullified.

"I don't know where these waivers came from, but they're unethical," said Thom Mayer, the union's medical director. "I know they go against the prime concept that we're going to do the right thing for the patient, not the right thing for the people who take care of the patient."

NFL spokesman Greg Aiello said that to the league's knowledge only one team physician distributed waivers, and the union has not requested a date for a hearing.

Because the NFL had no guidelines pertaining to Toradol usage, last year Matt Matava, the St. Louis Rams' team physician and president-elect of the NFL Physician's Society, took a closer look at the drug and its side effects, balancing the risks with the potential benefits. While his ensuing report noted that "each team physician is ultimately free to practice medicine as he or she feels is in the best interest of the patient," he issued a set of recommendations, including that Toradol shouldn't be used prophylactically; it should be limited to those with a known injury; it shouldn't be used in any form for more than five days; and it shouldn't be used concurrently with other NSAIDs.

"We just said, 'Listen, this is what the literature has suggested is out there, this is what our recommendations are based on the synthesis of the literature,'" Matava said. "'Do with Toradol as you see fit.'"

While Matava stopped short of advising 31 other team doctors to stop using Toradol, he has essentially eliminated the drug from his own locker room. In 2001, the Rams averaged six pregame Toradol injections, which increased to 16 over the next 10 seasons. Because use had become so widespread, Matava wasn't sure how players would react when he stopped administering the drug.

"We had two players come up to me at the very first game and said, 'I'm here for my Toradol shot,'" Matava recalled. "I said, 'We're not using it anymore.' 'Okay, can I have something else?' I never heard one more word about it the rest of the season."

The inconsistent use of prescription drugs from team to team highlights how varied practices can be across the league.

Matava said the NFL Physician's Society recently conducted a league-wide survey, and though he would not release the specific results, he said overall Toradol use last season was down. The survey was done anonymously, so the extent of Toradol usage from team to team is only known anecdotally. Teams such as the Rams, Packers, Falcons and Redskins, for example, say they avoid using the drug whenever possible.

"It's dramatically dropped," said Casolaro, the Redskins' doctor who has been with the team since 1999. "The truth is, I don't think it was ever a harm, nor do I still think it is."

Lapses in Standards

The inconsistent use of prescription drugs from team to team highlights how varied practices can be across the league. The NFL's protocols, standards and enforcement have not always been consistent with federal laws governing prescription drugs.

Many of the lapses in the league's complicated system were on display in the spring of 2009 in New Orleans. During a four-month stretch, the Saints' team trainers noticed Vicodin pills had gone missing. On April 28, 2009, according to a civil complaint later filed in state district court, the team's director of security, a former FBI agent named Geoffrey Santini, was notified. At the instruction of Saints General Manager Mickey Loomis, Santini installed a pair of hidden cameras in the Saints' training room.

Only a properly licensed pharmacy may store prescription drugs, and they must be properly secured and counted pill by pill in federally reported logs, according to DEA regulations.

The footage in the first video is in full color, grainy but unmistakable. Saints assistant head coach Joe Vitt, wearing khaki shorts and a black long-sleeved team shirt, can be seen unlocking a metal cabinet in the trainer's office. Unaware that he's being recorded, Vitt removes a bottle and pours pills into his hand before locking the cabinet and exiting the room.

There are two more video clips from the ensuing days that clearly show Vitt alone in the office, unlocking a cabinet and helping himself to a handful of prescription painkillers. The locks were quickly changed and one final video captured Vitt's failed attempt to get inside the cabinet.

Not long after, Santini called Loomis to discuss the situation and recorded the conversation. During the exchange, the two discussed to what authority they must answer.

"Mickey, I am just telling you that is not how it works," Santini says. "The law is there."

"We are not talking about the law," Loomis responds. "We are talking about the league."

The videos and recorded conversations, much of them reviewed by *The Post*, have become evidence in a DEA investigation that is now in the hands of the U.S. Attorney's office in New Orleans. The case is still open and, according to people with knowledge of the situation, federal authorities are weighing a hefty fine against the Saints for violating laws governing the proper storage, control and dispensing of prescription drugs.

Only a properly licensed pharmacy may store prescription drugs, and they must be properly secured and counted pill by pill in federally reported logs, according to DEA regulations. Only physicians can administer them. It is illegal for anyone else, including athletic trainers or coaches, to control or hand them out. In an effort to comply, the NFL subjects teams to annual pill audits, requiring them to report every dosage. But the system is far from fail-safe. In the Saints' training room, as the video showed, access to the drug cabinet was relatively unchecked and those with access could scoop out pills by the handful.

After Vitt was caught on camera, the team's trainers initially seemed to underappreciate the severity of what had happened and explained to Santini in recorded conversations that they intended to falsify the counts in their drug logs. "Our numbers will be right. . . . We are going back and adjusting, you know, these discrepancies and crediting" Vitt, Scottie Patton, the head trainer, told Santini.

Most teams now use a third-party company, registered with the DEA, that delivers prescription medication to team facilities and NFL stadiums, and maintain detailed drug logs. Using computer software, the substances can then be tracked by both the NFL and the third-party company. About half the NFL teams use a firm named SportPharm, and a spokeswoman for the company said several teams are mandated by the league to use its services to keep their operations in proper order.

In 2009, the Saints used a system that was a bit simpler. A Vicodin prescription by Saints team physician John Amoss was filled at a local Walgreens, according to court records, listing the patient as "New Orleans Saints."

The Saints declined to comment for this article or make Loomis, Vitt, Patton or Amoss available for comment. In a June 2009 recorded conversation, Loomis said Vitt was seeing a counselor and was in the care of a doctor. "We got him on the path of correction," he said. Loomis also made clear that he didn't think Vitt was abusing painkillers: "I am telling you what the doctor said: Joe is not a drug addict with a drug problem."

Despite earlier talk of falsifying records, in the recorded conversation, Santini appears to convince Loomis that the team would be violating the law and they'd all be subject to prosecution if they tried to fix the books or cover up the issue. "I'm not for breaking the law, I am for reporting this," the general manager said. "I'm also trying to do a solution that doesn't get Joe in a lot of hot water because I think we are on a path. This issue [is] corrected."

Vitt, who served as the Saints interim head coach last season, agreed in U.S. District Court to enter what's known as a pre-trial diversion program, a form of probation for first-time offenders in which he fulfilled certain obligations for 12 months, ranging from paying a fine to undergoing education, according to two people familiar with the agreement.

Santini resigned from the Saints organization on Aug. 16, 2009, and filed a lawsuit against the team eight months later. The case was moved to arbitration and the sides privately settled, but the allegations had already caught the eyes of federal authorities. Investigators with the DEA unearthed a number of violations with the Saints' operation, according to people familiar with the situation, and worked with the team to bring the organization into better compliance.

Search for Pain Relief

About five years ago, Casolaro, the Redskins' physician, said he learned of an Atlanta doctor who flew to the Washington area midweek to meet with and provide treatment for a Redskins player. Casolaro passed the information to league security, which informed the man he wasn't licensed to practice medicine in Virginia.

"He never came back," Casolaro said.

The incident highlights an age-old dilemma NFL medical personnel face. Team physicians who would like to rely less on pain medications wrestle with the alternative: The pain exists, therefore so does the need for painkillers. As Casolaro said, "If we don't give them a drug that they're allowed to have, will they go get it from outside? And what will they get?"

It's a legitimate concern: The Washington University School of Medicine study found that of players who misuse pain medication, 63 percent said they obtained their pills from a source other than a doctor.

The demand isn't spurred solely by a chemical addiction. Toradol isn't a narcotic, but the 2002 study of the drug's usage in the NFL found several teams reporting a "psychological addiction" to game-day injections.

"Because you rely so much on the instant pain relief," said Ibrahim, the D.C. United doctor, "people can become habituated to it."

Wilson Compton, a division director at the National Institute of Drug Abuse and a former clinician in the league's substance abuse program, says the reality is that NFL players simply deal with more pain than the average citizen. The

Washington University School of Medicine study found that only 13 percent of players reported their overall health to be excellent, while 81 percent reported feeling "moderate to severe" pain daily.

Compton was struck "by the quantity and extent of painful conditions the players who retired are experiencing. . . . This tells us that their bodies suffer extraordinary stress and disruption."

Further study is needed of what doctors and athletes are really using to treat pain, Compton says—how much are they using, and why? For instance, Compton asks, are players also seeking medication from their personal physicians?

"It's helpful to have research," he said, "so there really is some medical and health information about the long term, and it isn't just considering, 'What can I do to get through the next seven days?'"

Marijuana Can Play a Legitimate Role for Professional Football Players

Marvin Washington, Brendon Ayanbadejo, and Scott Fujita

Marvin Washington is a retired eleven-year NFL veteran and CTE/concussion advocate for retired players. Brendon Ayanbadejo played in the NFL for thirteen years and is currently an analyst/writer for Fox Sports. Scott Fujita played for eleven years and now works as an NFL broadcaster and sports writer. All three are Super Bowl champions.

Super Bowl week brings back fond memories for us. We shed a lot of blood, sweat and tears to earn our Super Bowl rings.

For years, we put our bodies in harm's way in the ultimate team sport, and for many of our NFL [National Football League] colleagues, the physical damage done in pursuit of our dreams is often permanent, and sometimes terribly debilitating.

The NFL is the preeminent sports league in the U.S. but it is woefully behind the curve when it comes to marijuana and players are suffering as a result. Many former and current NFL players use or have used marijuana to treat pain associated with injuries sustained on the field. There is a compelling body of research showing that marijuana can help treat pain and brain injuries.

Roughly a year ago, Commissioner Roger Goodell expressed a willingness to consider the medical use of marijuana for players if medical experts deem it a legitimate option. He said, "We'll continue to follow the medicine . . . that's something we would never take off the table if we could benefit our players at the end of the day."

The NFL should abandon its policy of drug testing and punishing players for use of marijuana.

It is time for Roger Goodell to make good on that promise. The NFL should lead the way in developing a more rational and science-based approach to marijuana. According to the Drug Policy Alliance, abundant evidence already exists regarding the medical potential and benefits of marijuana. Roughly half of the fifty states (representing nearly half of NFL markets) have legalized the use of marijuana for medical purposes, and over seventy percent of Americans support this reform. It just so happens that this week's [January 2015] Super Bowl is being played in Arizona, a state that allows the use of marijuana for medical purposes.

The NFL Should Promote Marijuana Research

First and foremost, the NFL should allocate financial resources to advance medical research on the efficacy of medical marijuana in treating brain injuries. In the case of trauma, a lot of inflammation occurs, which affects cognitive functioning and neural connectivity. A compound in marijuana called cannabidiol (CBD) has shown scientific potential to be an antioxidant and neuroprotectant for the brain. In a sport where closed head injuries are common, the league should be doing everything it can to help keep their players healthy during and after their careers. If the NFL wants to continue to grow its game, it must investigate potential medical solutions for its industrial disease, Chronic Traumatic Encephalopathy (CTE). Even the federal government holds a patent on marijuana for this purpose.

Second, the NFL should abandon its policy of drug testing and punishing players for use of marijuana. The NHL does not include marijuana among its banned substances and, just last week, the NCAA announced that it plans to re-examine its approach to drug testing student-athletes for non-performance enhancing drugs like marijuana because "they do not provide a competitive advantage." The HBO show "Real Sports with Bryant Gumbel" reported that 50-60 percent of players currently use marijuana regularly, mostly for pain relief. Solid evidence already indicates that such use can reduce reliance on opiate-based pain medications as well as anti-inflammatory drugs, many of which present pernicious side effects.

Addressing Enforcement Disparities

Finally, the NFL should take a leadership role in addressing racial disparities in marijuana law enforcement as well as other injustices caused by ineffective prohibitionist policies. Many players enjoy the use of marijuana apart from its medical benefits, just as tens of millions of other Americans do. A majority of Americans now favor regulating and taxing marijuana, more or less like alcohol, and four states have approved such policies, with more likely to do so in coming years. According to the ACLU [American Civil Liberties Union], African Americans are far more likely than other Americans to be arrested for marijuana possession even though they are no more likely to use or possess marijuana. This basic injustice should be of particular concern to the NFL given that more than two-thirds of all current players are African American.

As former NFL players, we recognize our role as leaders and role models. We firmly believe that reforming marijuana policies can, indeed must, go hand in hand with discouraging young people from using marijuana and other drugs. There is no place any longer, either in the NFL or the nation at large, for the injustices and hypocrisies of prohibitionist marijuana policies. It's time for the NFL to be a leader and create a rational and science-based marijuana policy.

CHAPTER 4

What Are Some Other Key Issues with Professional Football?

Chapter Preface

With the NFL making headlines for so many things besides its game-day action, it's no surprise that most stories appear in the media spotlight only briefly before being eclipsed by other items of interest. The public has a short attention span for most things, but sometimes, as folks in the news business say, a story "has legs." That means the original story continues to generate interest as related follow-up issues keep it relevant in the public mind.

Such is certainly the case with the issue of concussions and chronic traumatic encephalopathy (CTE) in the NFL. The original story linking blows sustained on the field with long-term cognitive disability generated intense media coverage; that story gained further traction when news surfaced about players filing a class-action lawsuit over the issue and the NFL's eventual financial settlement; those stories were then superseded by coverage of NFL rule changes intended to reduce the frequency of head and neck strikes and blind hits on defenseless players. (Ball-carriers are now banned from lowering their helmets into defenders as they try to break a tackle, tackling has been eliminated during preseason practices, and the kickoff spot has been moved forward so more kicks go into the end zone for a touchback instead of being caught and returned by the receiving team; kickoff returns cause more concussions than any other play in football.)

But the NFL concussion story hasn't ended there, either. It has since evolved to include complex and passionate debates over whether and how to make football safer, whether the new rules actually protect players or just give the illusion that the league is making meaningful safety improvements, and whether fans are complicit in the problem.

Along with increased public awareness of the CTE issue, media coverage has also increased player awareness. Another developing story is the slow but steady stream of young, healthy players who are walking away from the NFL, some—like San Francisco 49er's standout linebacker Chris Borland—after only playing one pro season.

"He's 24 years old and the first player to retire directly because he wanted to avoid the traumatic brain injuries that have been linked to playing football,"[1] noted CNN shortly after Borland's announcement in March 2015.

"Players walking away from football, rather than trying their luck with [repeated concussions], is a good sign," writes Gregg Easterbrook in his recent book *The King of Sports: Football's Impact on America*. "But much more reform is needed for concussion management during games and for the penalizing of helmet-to-helmet hits."[2]

Easterbrook goes on to list a dozen key reforms that could make football significantly safer, some of which are echoed by Jeff Nussbaum in his viewpoint in this chapter. Others, however, cautiously disagree and say that if football's risks are reduced too much, the game will lose its intensity and become a shadow of its former self.

"All of these changes are designed to make the game safer for the players," writes Marc Tracy in the *New Republic*. "At the same time, all disadvantage particular types of players (respectively: running backs, who can no longer gain extra yardage by lowering their helmets; kick-returners, whose jobs just got less prestigious; and linebackers as well as defenders generally, who can't practice tackling technique). And all raise

1. Roxanne Jones, "Why Are These NFLers Retiring Early?," CNN, March 17, 2015. http://www.cnn.com/2015/03/12/opinions/jones-nfl-early-retirement/index.html.

2. Gregg Easterbrook, *The King of Sports: Football's Impact on America*, New York: St. Martin's Press, 2013, p. 170.

a question that, one worries, the league ... is not thinking carefully enough about: What makes football football?"[3]

While the NFL (and its fans) endeavors to answer that question, CNN notes that the early retirement trend means that "maybe there is another way out [besides suicide] for young players who are now better informed about the dangers of the game. Just maybe all the debates about the ugly side of football—concussions, brain injuries, depression and suicides—have done some good, after all."[4]

The issue of concussions and CTE in the NFL continues to have legs and is likely to keep drawing attention for quite some time. The authors in this chapter present a wide array of viewpoints that consider the ongoing issues of player safety, the fairness of the NFL concussion lawsuit settlement, the morality of watching and supporting pro football, the economic impacts of the game, the NFL's longtime nonprofit status, and the allure of playing Fantasy Football.

3. Marc Tracy, "NFL Rules Changes: When Is Football No Longer Football?," *New Republic*, August 2, 2013. http://www.newrepublic.com/article/114148/nfl-rules-changes-when-football-no-longer-football.

4. Roxanne Jones, op cit.

Three Simple Fixes That Could Save Pro Football: Reimagining the Game for the Twenty-First Century

Jeff Nussbaum

Jeff Nussbaum is a partner in the speechwriting and strategy firm West Wing Writers. He has previously advised leagues, teams, and professional athletes.

On the afternoon of November 25, 1905, a sophomore on the Union College football team named Harold Moore plunged headlong into New York University's offensive wedge in an effort to "buck the line" and stop NYU's running back. If Moore wore any protective equipment at all, it was likely a nose guard or a padded hat. Players did wear "wedge belts," which allowed teammates to hold on to each other and plow forward as a unit.

The football played in 1905 would be nearly unrecognizable today. The distance required for a first down was five yards, making just about every play a "mass" play, in which the entire offense tried to inch forward by any means necessary. Forward passes were illegal. Dropkicks and punches, while considered ungentlemanly, were not. Falling on the ball didn't stop a play, but rather initiated a prolonged pileup underneath which lawlessness reigned.

As Moore attempted to tackle the ball carrier, his head was hit by the knee of one of his teammates, knocking him unconscious. Though he was seen at Fordham Hospital that afternoon, they had no means of detecting the cerebral hemorrhage he had suffered. Moore died that evening. He was one of an estimated twenty college football players to die that season—and one of three to die *that day.*

It is time to once again make significant changes to the way [football] is played and the way the league is governed.

A flurry of emergency meetings took place among college presidents and coaches. President Theodore Roosevelt got involved, gathering football coaches and officials at the White House to discuss "[s]uch modifications of the rules as would eliminate its brutal features," as the *Washington Post* reported at the time.

> In September of 1906, the new rules were published. They included the forward pass, three plays to achieve a first down, a neutral zone between the offense and the defense at the beginning of each play, and penalties for unnecessary roughness. (Less noted, but equally important, the new rules also recommended "football armor," including knee pads, and thigh pads "sewn inside the trousers.") George H. Brooke, Swarthmore's coach, summarized the new rules thusly: "There will certainly be a great deal more kicking, flukes, passing, tricks, open field running and general hurry scurry."

Even before the sweeping rule changes in 1906, there was concern in some quarters that any changes would alter the game to the point at which it became unrecognizable and, worse, unmasculine. The artist Frederick Remington summed up these concerns in a letter to the legendary Walter Camp: "Football, in my opinion, is best at its worst. I do not believe in all its namby-pamby talk, and I hope the game will not be emasculated and robbed of its heroic qualities. People who don't like football as now played might like [the card game] whist—advise them to try that."

Despite opinions like Remington's, however, the new rules went into effect. The National Football League was founded in 1920, playing the game under those new rules. Today, that "hurry scurry" has made professional football the most popular sport in America for thirty straight years.

The safer game thrived. A century later, many fewer players are dying on the field. But many more, due largely to the effects of repeated concussions and chronic traumatic encephalopathy (CTE), are dying—and, it appears, killing—because of it. It is time to once again make significant changes to the way the game is played and the way the league is governed. Just as the game was radically reimagined in the early twentieth century, it needs to be reimagined for the twenty-first.

Here are three changes that would do just that.

Starting from a two-point stance not only reduces helmet-to-helmet contact, but it also values speed and agility over pure mass, both of which make the game safer for those who play it.

#1 Do away with the three-point stance

In 1994, when Ralph Isernia was coaching at Methodist University in North Carolina, he came to a realization. If he took his lineman out of the traditional three-point stance, in which the player starts in a squatting position with his hand on the ground, it opened up a number of options. For starters, according to Isernia, "[i]n a three point stance, they're looking [up] through their eyebrows or just seeing feet." In his version of a two-point stance, which he calls the "attack two-point stance," his offensive linemen could see where they'd have to make a block and where blitzes were coming from.

Because of the rules of football, the two-point stance confers another advantage. Once a lineman puts his hand to the ground, the rules require that he remain motionless until the ball is snapped and the play begins. Defenses are not required to do this, and thus can alter their positioning at any point. With two-point stances, offensive players are allowed to adjust their distance from each other (their "splits") so long as they stand still for one second before the play begins—which makes it easier to change plays in response to the defense.

In the two decades since making his discovery, Coach Isernia has developed a reputation as someone who can turn lackluster offenses into scoring machines. Isernia has just completed his second season at RPI. Previously, as the offensive coordinator at Ferrum College, he helped mold two different quarterbacks into conference players of the year. Prior to that, at the University of Charleston, he led an offense that was a league leader in scoring, rushing, and passing efficiency. He compares the three-point stance to a Nolan Ryan fastball—all power—and the two-point stance to a Mariano Rivera cutter—fast but with movement. When his teams began using the two-point stance exclusively (many teams employ it in clear passing situations), people would ask him after games what his philosophy was, and he would outline the advantages as he saw them.

Today, it's becoming clear that the two-point stance confers perhaps an even more meaningful advantage. In all of the discussions about concussions and CTE, one of the statistics most frequently trotted out by the NFL is that a woman soccer player is two and a half times more likely to suffer what researchers call a "frank" concussion—a concussion caused by a single blow to the head—than a college football player. While this may be true, what this statistic and several others of its ilk conveniently neglect is that frank concussions are only one piece of the larger CTE problem. The most recent science indicates that the accumulation of separate subconcussive hits is as damaging as a single frank concussion. And the vast majority of those hits take place in the trenches, between offensive and defensive linemen who start in a low stance and fire up and at each other when the ball is snapped. For most linemen, this fierce helmet-to-helmet collision takes place on nearly every play.

However, when linemen begin plays upright, in a two-point stance, they engage each other's hands, arms, and shoulders first, and helmet-to-helmet contact is often incidental. Watch Coach Isernia's teams and you see fast, nimble linemen who behave more like running backs, seeking openings in the defense and using speed, positioning, and leverage to open holes. What were once called the trenches become yet another series of finesse positions. Starting from a two-point stance not only reduces helmet-to-helmet contact, but it also values speed and agility over pure mass, both of which make the game safer for those who play it.

#2 Demand better helmets

Football fans of a certain age will remember Don Beebe. A wide receiver for the Buffalo Bills in their heyday in the late 1980s and early 1990s, he was an inspiration to five-foot-eleven white kids like me. Beebe was fast and tenacious. He was also a magnet for ferocious hits. After sustaining several concussions, he and teammate Mark Kelso began wearing their helmets with a special covering that was fitted onto the existing helmet, called a ProCap. This technology put padding on the outside of the helmet, giving the helmets a puffy, inflated look (they were frequently referred to as "Gazoo" helmets, after the *Flintstones* character). But the covering also served to dissipate the energy of helmet-to-helmet hits by 30 percent. A small study of the technology, conducted at St. Alban's High School in Washington, D.C., by George Washington University's sports medicine department, had half the players wear ProCap coverings and half stick with their traditional helmets. There were no concussions among ProCap users, and six among those who didn't use it. Kelso never had another concussion after he started to use a ProCap. Other players began using the helmets as well.

This is where NFL helmet politics come into play. The NFL claims to be a helmet democracy, in which players are allowed to choose any helmet they like. In practice, this means that an overwhelming number of them choose helmets made by Riddell, the NFL's official helmet sponsor. Because Riddell has the imprimatur of the NFL, younger players tend to choose their helmets and stick with them as they rise through the football ranks. And many players admit they choose helmets for aesthetic reasons, assuming safety to be equal among them. But the major flaw with today's NFL helmets is that their design is a vestige of a time in which skull fractures were a greater concern than concussions.

As helmet-testing regimes have improved, results show that Riddell is the maker of some of the best and worst models in terms of concussion prevention.

In 1996, Riddell effectively signed the ProCap's death warrant, stating that Riddell's warranty would be negated if their helmets were modified with the use of the ProCap.

Riddell maintained that wearers of the ProCap were at a greater risk for neck and spinal injuries, because of the concern that two padded helmets hitting one another would maintain contact long enough to put players in danger of "axial loading," spinal damage caused by a blow to the top of the head. Despite studies showing that this was not the case, the warning went to youth sports equipment dealers and college customers, and the ProCap all but disappeared. Other helmet innovations met similar fates, as the league, Riddell, and the league's then-laughable concussion committee disparaged and denigrated these new models.

More recently, as helmet-testing regimes have improved, results show that Riddell is the maker of some of the best and worst models in terms of concussion prevention. Players at all levels need to know which helmets are the best, and the worst, irrespective of brand. For the league to regain credibility with players and make players safer, it should cease to have a helmet sponsor. Taking self-interest out of the equation would allow the league to conduct unbiased helmet safety and impact ratings, and make those ratings available to all players. If one model of helmet proves to be clearly superior in protecting against injury and concussion (as the ProCap might), the league could even mandate use of that helmet.

Would future helmets look different than today's? Perhaps. Would they even seem silly, by today's standards? Quite possibly. Would the more flexible helmets that seem to fare better in safety tests diminish the satisfying crack of a big hit? Likely. But could they represent a change that would make the game safer for players at all levels? Without a doubt.

#3 Make guaranteed contracts the norm

In 2012, the New England Patriots signed a tight end named Aaron Hernandez to a five-year, $40 million contract. Hernandez had a troubled history. In 2007, during his first year in college, he was involved in a brawl that required a police response and later that year was questioned in a shooting. Two weeks before signing that $40 million contract, he was involved in a double homicide for which he is now being investigated. After signing the contract, he was involved in another shooting for which he is now being sued. And then in June 2013, he was arrested in the fatal shooting of a man named Odin Lloyd, with whom he was acquainted. Ninety minutes after that arrest, the Patriots released Hernandez, and owed him nothing on the $40 million contract beyond what had already been paid.

NFL contracts aren't true contracts, at least not by any standard definition of a contract. Players can be cut at any time, for virtually any reason—including injury. Clearly, this is bad for players. But what the NFL needs to realize is that it creates a serious incentive misalignment that is hurting the league and its players. First, it encourages teams to push players to and through injury, rather than investing in their long-term health. Additionally, it allows teams to sign "riskier" players and then jettison them if things don't go well.

Guaranteed contracts can serve a forcing function to get teams to operate in the league's interest, by policing their own players, treating or reforming them where necessary, and working to keep them healthy.

If the Patriots knew they'd be on the hook for the full $40 million no matter what, would they have signed Hernandez? Not without looking more deeply into his background. If a team is going to sign someone with a history of domestic abuse with the knowledge that they'll have to pay out the full contract, you can bet they'll make sure that player gets counseling and support. And if a team signs any player to a long-term contract, they're going to be much more committed to that player's long-term physical and mental health.

When the Minnesota Vikings announced they would start star running back Adrian Peterson despite his indictment on charges of child abuse, they were acting in their own interest: they wanted their best player on the field. Guaranteed contracts can serve a forcing function to get teams to operate in the league's interest, by policing their own players, treating or reforming them where necessary, and working to keep them healthy.

Yes, football remains a giant athwart the American professional sporting scene. But there are cracks in the NFL's vaunted shield. According to Jeetendr Sehdev, a professor at the University of Southern California and the author of *Superstar: The Art and Science of Celebrity Branding*, the NFL's brand now performs in the lowest 10 percent of 200 brands across four of the seven most important factors of trust: openness, acceptance, compassion, and consistency. Its appeal is particularly suffering among women and millennials, and youth football participation is down. Significantly, these trends were all apparent even before a season that has brought us a glaring case of domestic violence (which led to the belated publicity of several other cases of domestic violence among league players), one of the league's biggest stars being suspended for child abuse, and the arrest of more than thirty NFL players on a variety of charges (as of mid-December).

In June 1904, speaking on the subject of "higher ideals" to Harvard's graduating class, Teddy Roosevelt turned to the topic of injuries in football: "When these injuries are inflicted wantonly, or of set design," he said, "we are confronted by a question not of damage to one man's body, but of another man's character."

The injuries suffered by today's NFL are injuries inflicted by set design: an unwillingness on the part of the league to honestly confront the challenges that its own rules, structures, and customs have put in place. But if league officials are willing to embrace changes like the three outlined above, teams of the future won't have to brag that they were playing the best football when the last football was played, but rather that they were able to help evolve the game to become a permanently sustainable activity.

Professional Football Is Good for the Economy

Yuval Rosenberg

Yuval Rosenberg is executive editor of Fiscal Times, *an online publication that focuses on business news and analysis.*

The gladiators of the gridiron are back. The National Football League (NFL) officially kicked off its 94th season Thursday night [September 5, 2013], but Sunday brings its first full slate of games—and with it, a full-fledged revving of the economic engine that is America's favorite, and most profitable, sport.

Commissioner Roger Goodell has set an aggressive goal of getting the league to $25 billion in revenue by 2027. It has a long way to go, but is clearly ahead of other major sports. The NFL generated $9.5 billion in revenues in 2012, some $2 billion more than Major League Baseball. The 32 teams themselves are worth more than $37 billion combined, according to *Forbes.*

The NFL's revenue includes $4 billion from television broadcast rights contracts with the likes of CBS, ESPN, Fox, NBC and satellite provider DirecTV. Those TV revenues are set to go up to $5 billion starting next year. The league can attract such TV prices because its games consistently draw strong ratings, particularly with viewers in the 18- to 49-year old demographic group that advertisers covet. The Super Bowl, of course, gets monster viewership year after year, but regular season and even preseason games consistently get millions of fans to watch—and watch live, when they're more likely to see ads that they might skip on a recorded program.

NBC's "Sunday Night Football" was the top-rated show among those viewers over the 2012–2013 television season, though it was beaten out by CBS drama "NCIS" among viewers overall.

Fantasy football is a massively popular phenomenon that cannot be ignored.

Widespread Economic Impact

Yet the league's current economic impact reaches well beyond its own TV deals or sales of tickets and merchandise. It extends to sales of everything from beer and chicken wings to flat-screen TVs and high-end sound systems. Chances are, it even extends to your office. Once a subculture for dedicated stathead fans, fantasy sports have exploded in popularity, with football leading the way. More than 25 million Americans played fantasy football last year, spending more than $3 billion on league entry fees and other related content and services, including stuff like this.

Outplacement firm Challenger, Gray & Christmas noted in a press release last week [September 2013] that it may be virtually impossible to calculate the productivity costs of millions of workers minding their teams on company time—but that didn't deter the firm from taking a stab at it anyway. Using government data on average hourly earnings and assuming employees work on their teams for an hour a week, the firm roughly estimated a productivity hit of nearly $8.3 billion over a full fantasy season, even while acknowledging their math might be meaningless—and that a little time spent on a fantasy team could improve office morale and overall worker productivity.

"So, what's the point of this non-scientific study?" CEO John Challenger asked in the release. "It is simply to acknowledge that fantasy football is a massively popular phenomenon that cannot be ignored."

By the Numbers

34: Percentage of fans who said that pro football was their favorite sport in a January poll by Harris Interactive, compared with 24 percent who chose pro football in 1985. Baseball was a distant second in the most recent poll, with 16 percent calling it their favorite.

17,303,347: Regular season attendance at NFL games in 2012, according to *Sports Business Journal*, up from 2011 but down from 17,605,811 in 2006.

$2.3 Billion: Value of the Dallas Cowboys, according to *Forbes*. The team had operating income of more than $250 million.

$825 Million: Value of the Oakland Raiders, the lowest of any franchise in the NFL.

$3.5 Million: Operating loss last season for the Detroit Lions, the only team in the league to be in the red, according to *Forbes*.

$1.1 Billion: Value of the five-year contract agreed to by Nike in 2012 to become the NFL's official uniform provider.

$1 Billion: Value of the four-year contract agreed to by Verizon Wireless in June to live-stream NFL games. The deal takes effect in 2014.

17: Number of billionaires among the league's 31 owners (with the Green Bay Packers being publicly owned).

[Approximately 110,000] jobs across various industries [are] supported by the NFL, according to a 2011 story by the Associated Press.

$29.5 Million: Compensation paid by the league to Commissioner Roger Goodell in 2011, more than many CEOs of Fortune 500 companies received.

501(c)(6): Section of the tax code that explicitly grants professional football leagues that are not organized for profit a tax exemption. The NFL league office does not pay taxes because of that exemption, written into law in 1966, but the 32 individual teams do. Sen. Tom Coburn (R-OK) has proposed to end that exemption.

110,000: Approximate number of jobs across various industries supported by the NFL, according to a 2011 story by the Associated Press.

$765 million: Amount the NFL agreed to pay over 20 years to settle a lawsuit brought by 4,500 former players who accused the league of concealing information it had about the long-term risks of concussions. The league did not admit to any wrongdoing in agreeing to the settlement, which must still be approved by a federal judge.

1,496: Injuries that sidelined a player for eight or more days during the 2012 season, up 37 percent from 1,095 in the 2009 season, according to an analysis of NFL data by Edgeworth Economics.

$22,344,408: Compensation due for the 2013 season to 24 NFL players who had torn their anterior cruciate ligaments as of mid-August, according to Spotrac. All but one of the players are expected to miss the full season.

Hosting a Super Bowl Is a Bad Deal for Cities

Alan Pyke

Alan Pyke is the deputy economic policy editor for ThinkProgress .org at the Center for American Progress Action Fund, a progressive public policy research and advocacy organization.

When Tom Brady and Richard Sherman square off in Super Bowl XLIX on Sunday [February 1, 2015] in Glendale, AZ, the city of 230,000 will be in the home stretch of its week-long hosting duties. But the huge expenses of becoming a magnet for big events in sports will linger.

It is the second time Glendale has hosted the NFL's [National Football League] championship circus, and the city is deep in debt thanks to its effort to become a professional athletics hub. Multiple layers of complex financing arrangements around three separate sports spaces in town have starved the suburb of resources it needs to provide services to its people, and this week's festivities will worsen Glendale's problems. Being vocal about what his town is paying for its hosting privileges may have cost Mayor Jerry Weiers a chance to even watch the game in person.

Weiers' reservations make plenty of sense when you look at Glendale's sporting pursuits through the perspective of the city's dire economic straits. Here are six numbers that take some air out of the rosy economic projections used to justify the game.

125 Homeless People

Glendale's homeless population was estimated to be 125 last January. One study in Florida has estimated that it would cost about $10,000 per year to provide permanent housing and services to a homeless person. That means the $2 or $3 million Glendale is spending on Super Bowl security alone could more than cover the $1.25 million cost of ending its homelessness problem for a year.

Unable to extricate itself from the stadium deals or win sufficient concessions from the relevant teams and leagues, Glendale had to cut where it could.

$40.5 Million

Even if the state or the league were to reimburse Glendale's security costs—which they won't—that money wouldn't necessarily be freed up for social services. That's because Glendale spends a combined $40.5 million each year on debt, upkeep, and leases related to its two other, non-football stadiums. The first and most expensive of these is the Phoenix Coyotes hockey arena, a desert ice palace that has driven Glendale deep into debt and forced significant cuts to public services in the Phoenix suburb. The second is a spring training baseball park for the Chicago White Sox and the Los Angeles Dodgers. A state agency currently pays the equivalent annual costs for the football stadium, but a legal battle is threatening to derail the state tourism tax levy that supports that arrangement. If the state loses that case, Glendale could eventually be on the hook for another $12 million in annual stadium costs. Even as the Arizona Sports and Tourism Authority waits for the fallout from that case, it's paying the NFL $4 million to refund sales taxes tied to Super Bowl tickets.

70 Percent

Glendale's stadium spending each year could cover seven out of every 10 dollars that Arizona as a whole spent administering food stamps to nearly 477,000 households. The benefits themselves are federally funded, but states split the administrative tab with the federal government. Arizona's share of those costs was $58 million in 2013. It's easy to get lost in abstractions around the stadium's impact on Glendale's municipal finances, but this comparison makes it concrete: for what the city is spending, Arizona could provide food assistance to 333,000 low-income households a year.

1 in 5 City Workers

Glendale officials estimate the city has cut its public workforce by 20 percent since the recession. Prior to the housing market crash, Glendale's debt-financed stadiums had kept more-or-less afloat. But when the downturn pummeled the Arizona suburbs, a series of financial arrangements that had just about worked in good times became untenable—and inescapable. Unable to extricate itself from the stadium deals or win sufficient concessions from the relevant teams and leagues, Glendale had to cut where it could. In 2012, the City Council simultaneously cut 49 public service jobs and approved a lease agreement to pay any future owner of the struggling Coyotes hockey franchise a cool $15 million annually. The city threatened to close public facilities and cut another 250 employees, including first responders, if voters didn't approve a sales tax hike intended to help fill in the city's budget hole.

3.7 Billion Taxpayer Dollars

The online for-profit education company University of Phoenix paid $155 million to put its name on Glendale's football stadium in 2006. In 2012 alone, the company pulled in $3.7 billion from taxpayers. Sunday's Super Bowl might draw scrutiny back to the for-profit college sector thanks to the branding of the building. The naming rights cost the University of Phoenix about double what the company paid to settle a whistleblower lawsuit over its deceptive recruiter practices, but just pennies compared to the billions that companies like it spend marketing for-profit college degrees more directly each year.

$1.6 Million

That's what Glendale lost, on net, from hosting the 2008 Super Bowl. Despite boosters' claims that the game brings huge economic benefits, the city's last experience as a championship town confirms what actual economists say about these deals. "With these mega-events, yeah, you'll have people coming, staying at hotels, going to bars and restaurants," Minnesota State University-Mankato economics professor Phil Miller told ThinkProgress' Travis Waldron. "But then they go, and, OK, show's over. It doesn't leave behind much of a lasting impact. And it's a very narrow impact."

The NFL Should Be Stripped of Its Nonprofit Status

Andy Kroll

Andy Kroll is a senior reporter at Mother Jones *magazine. His work has also appeared in the* Wall Street Journal, *the* Guardian, Men's Journal, American Prospect, *and TomDispatch.com, where he is an associate editor.*

Times are good for the National Football League (NFL). Viewership is up. For the 47th year in a row, Harris Interactive named pro football the most popular sport in America. And with overall revenues north of $9 billion, the NFL is the most lucrative sports league on the planet.

That's not enough for NFL Commissioner Roger Goodell. He wants to nearly triple the league's revenues to $25 billion by 2027—a mind-bogglingly large number. But here's an even more shocking fact: The NFL pays nothing in taxes on all those revenues. Not a nickel. And now the anti-corruption organization Rootstrikers wants to put an end to the NFL's free ride.

Over the weekend [December 14, 2013], Rootstrikers blasted out an email urging people to sign a petition in support of Sen. Tom Coburn's (R-Okla.) PRO Sports Act, which would ban big sports leagues from receiving tax-exempt status. "You know the NFL as the National Football League," says the Rootstrikers email. "But the IRS knows them better as the Nonprofit Football League—that's because the NFL has not paid any taxes since 1966 and average Americans are left paying higher taxes to make up for that lost revenue. Senator [Tom] Coburn is trying to change that, and we support his endeavor." Coburn's bill would ban pro sports leagues with more than $10 million in revenue from receiving tax-exempt status.

The NFL isn't just ducking taxes; it's fleecing working people who do pay their taxes.

How Did the NFL Become a Nonprofit?

So, you might ask, how did the NFL score such a lucky deal in the first place? It's a classic tale of political influence and lobbying ingenious, as Gregg Easterbrook explains in an excerpt of his book *The King of Sports: Football's Impact on America*, published in the *Atlantic*:

> The 1961 Sports Broadcasting Act was the first piece of gift-wrapped legislation, granting the leagues legal permission to conduct television-broadcast negotiations in a way that otherwise would have been price collusion. Then, in 1966, Congress enacted Public Law 89-800, which broadened the limited antitrust exemptions of the 1961 law. Essentially, the 1966 statute said that if the two pro-football leagues of that era merged—they would complete such a merger four years later, forming the current NFL—the new entity could act as a monopoly regarding television rights. Apple or ExxonMobil can only dream of legal permission to function as a monopoly: the 1966 law was effectively a license for NFL owners to print money. Yet this sweetheart deal was offered to the NFL in exchange only for its promise not to schedule games on Friday nights or Saturdays in autumn, when many high schools and colleges play football.
>
> Public Law 89-800 had no name—unlike, say, the catchy USA Patriot Act or the Patient Protection and Affordable Care Act. Congress presumably wanted the bill to be low-profile, given that its effect was to increase NFL owners' wealth at the expense of average people.

While Public Law 89-800 was being negotiated with congressional leaders, NFL lobbyists tossed in the sort of obscure provision that is the essence of the lobbyist's art. The phrase "or professional football leagues" was added to Section 501(c)6 of 26 U.S.C., the Internal Revenue Code. Previously, a sentence in Section 501(c)6 had granted not-for-profit status to "business leagues, chambers of commerce, real-estate boards, or boards of trade." Since 1966, the code has read: "business leagues, chambers of commerce, real-estate boards, boards of trade, or professional football leagues."

The insertion of professional football leagues into the definition of not-for-profit organizations was a transparent sell-out of public interest. This decision has saved the NFL uncounted millions in tax obligations, which means that ordinary people must pay higher taxes, public spending must decline, or the national debt must increase to make up for the shortfall. Nonprofit status applies to the NFL's headquarters, which administers the league and its all-important television contracts. Individual teams are for-profit and presumably pay income taxes—though because all except the Green Bay Packers are privately held and do not disclose their finances, it's impossible to be sure.

Since winning that insanely lucrative add-in, the NFL has spent lavishly to protect it and keep lawmakers happy. The organization has shelled out $12.7 million on lobbying since 1998—more than any other professional sports league—and given $2 million in campaign donations since 1992, according to the Center for Responsive Politics.

A Profitable Enterprise

Those calling for the NFL to be stripped of its tax-exempt status point out that its leadership is making Wall Street money. In 2011, the NFL paid its five highest-ranking executives almost $60 million. Goodell alone pocketed $29 million. This largesse comes largely on the backs of taxpayers in cities that have pro football teams. As Easterbrook notes, "Judith Grant Long, a Harvard University professor of urban planning, calculates that league-wide, 70 percent of the capital cost of NFL stadiums has been provided by taxpayers, not NFL owners. Many cities, counties, and states also pay the stadiums' ongoing costs, by providing power, sewer services, other infrastructure, and stadium improvements." In other words, the NFL isn't just ducking taxes; it's fleecing working people who do pay their taxes.

To be clear, as the NFL points out, much of pro football's billions in revenue ultimately get funneled to the league's 32 teams, which do pay taxes. Yet the league office's 2011 revenues still add up to a staggering $255 million, while the league spent some $332 million that year.

Which brings us back to the Rootstrikers petition in support of Coburn's PRO Sports Act. The bill, which has been stuck in committee since September, could use all the help it can get. So as you settle onto the couch next Sunday for a full day of gridiron action, don't be fooled by the NFL's manly, to-the-victor-go-the-spoils ethos. The league is one of the biggest welfare queens around.

Editor's Note: In a letter to team owners dated April 28, 2015, NFL Commissioner Roger Goodell said the league will give up its tax-exempt status beginning with the 2015 tax season.

The Moral Case Against Football

Melissa Jeltsen

Melissa Jeltsen is a senior editor at The Huffington Post.

Is it immoral to consume violent entertainment that can result in dire, even deadly consequences for its participants? Is it immoral to cheer for a dazzling show knowing it could cause its stars to develop dementia or memory loss or depression?

That is to say, is it immoral to watch football?

In a punchy new manifesto, *New York Times* bestselling author Steve Almond argues that it is.

"This book is partly an attempt to say, 'Something is off here,'" Almond said in an interview with *The Huffington Post.* "Why is our most popular form of entertainment this unnecessarily violent, degrading spectacle that churns through the players who play it?"

Almond didn't want to have to write this story. A diehard football fan since he was 6 years old, he spent the last few decades rationalizing his love of the game so he could keep on enjoying it. But as a growing body of research linked head injuries to cognitive issues such as dementia, Alzheimer's and depression, it became harder and harder for him to ignore his conscience.

In his latest book, *Against Football,* Almond explains why he is ditching the sport for good. His moral qualms with football are multifaceted. There is the toll football takes on the players' bodies and brains. There is what Almond calls the NFL's [National Football League] nihilistic greed: "Do they feel no shame in snatching taxpayer money they don't really need from impoverished communities?" he writes. But beyond that, Almond worries that football negatively influences America's attitudes about violence, hyper-masculinity, racism and homophobia.

Time for Soul Searching

Throughout the book, he appeals to fellow fans to consider football's moral complexities before kicking back and enjoying the show.

I want people to confront the darker aspects of the game that they really don't want to face.

"I think there's a silent majority of football fans who feel increasingly queasy about watching it," he said. "There's a fundamental moral crisis of decision that individual fans have to make: Can I sponsor this game?"

By coming down hard on America's favorite game, Almond is wading into dangerous territory. Yes, the NFL has had a lot of bad press in the last few years, but that has not dented its popularity one bit. In a recent survey conducted by the Harris Poll, the NFL ranked as the most popular American sport for the 30th consecutive year in a row. The 2014 Super Bowl was the most watched TV show in U.S. history, with 111.5 million viewers tuning in.

But as a true devotee of the game, Almond is well-positioned to deliver the blow. In each line of the book, his genuine love of the sport shines through.

A Reluctant Messenger

"I didn't want to write a book that was looking down on football. I wanted to write a book about the hold, the grip that football has on people like me," he said. "I want people to confront the darker aspects of the game that they really don't want to face. I know that because I didn't want to face it for 40 years."

For Almond, it took a personal brush with brain trauma to realize he could no longer mindlessly enjoy football.

Two years ago, his mother fell in an accident and developed acute dementia. When Almond visited her in the ICU, she didn't even know who he was.

"People talk about the soul or the spirit being in our heart. No; it's in our brains," he said. "The brain makes you who you are. When that's gone, you're gone."

After seeing his mother in such a condition, brain trauma was no longer an abstraction.

"Once you see how devastating it is, it becomes much harder to put the genie back in the bottle and say, 'Let's just have some chicken wings and watch the game,'" he said. "We haven't even caught up to what the real medical risks are."

This football season will be the first time since Almond was a child that he will not be watching the NFL. While the book doesn't ask fans to boycott football, it implores them to take a closer look at what exactly they are supporting.

An Inconvenient Truth

"America is good at making us feel OK with things we really shouldn't feel OK about," he says. "It's what we've done for years with cigarettes, what is still done with our consumption of fossil fuels and meat. It's all about giving people the pleasure and airbrushing out of the picture the moral costs."

He says people who believe the game can't change are simply cynical. "That is what people always say," he said. "Moral progress is inconvenient. It requires people taking stock of their own behaviors and making inconvenient decisions that are hard in the short term and beneficial in the long term. America as a rule sucks at it but can be very good at it when sufficiently roused."

And that's the point of his book.

"Football is a remarkably exciting game, but it also reinforces a lot of basic American pathologies around race, violence, greed, sexuality, sexual orientation, and we give a free pass," he says. "We don't even think of it as something that deserves moral scrutiny, when it's the biggest thing in America. And that's nuts."

Actually, Anybody Can Play

Bindu Khurana

Bindu Khurana is a marriage and family therapist and adjunct faculty member at Argosy University in California.

The images of football have remained constant for years. Tailgating fans moving into sold-out stadiums in hopes of watching their favorite team light up the scoreboard in victory. However, pigskin adherents have shifted some of their loyalty into a new gridiron hybrid: fantasy football, which has taken the sports world by storm, with even commentators discussing how many fantasy points a player has just gotten his lucky owner.

Fantasy football is made up of a league of individuals who draft players to create their own teams. For some, this is a structured affair comprised of statistical analysis, thorough research of depth charts, and injury reports, as well as a detailed review of the rookie class. Others treat the draft as an opportunity to catch up with friends, as you sit around trying to get the best available players to be part of your team.

The deciding factor on strategy oftentimes depends on the cost to join. A league is created with a commissioner in charge of adding teams (individuals), setting up the rules, and scheduling a draft date and time. When the league is created, individuals now are owners of their team, assigning a team name and logo while attempting to get prime players on their roster. Now, football season truly has begun.

The next several weeks can be a tumultuous ride of emotions managing player injuries, bye weeks, and the omnipresent trash talk by fellow owners. Fantasy owners feel compelled to explain personnel decisions of benching or starting players similar to a head coach at a press conference. Each week an owner must decide who to start, with an eye on setting up the best matchups while also looking to fill gaps caused by injury or underperforming players.

Fantasy football can provide an escape from our daily lives.

Most leagues are pay-to-play circuits; each owner puts up an entry fee in the hopes of winning a bundle in the end. So, obviously, people play fantasy football to win extra money, but that is not the entire story.

Fantasy football allows a larger segment of society to feel engaged and part of one of this country's oldest and most celebrated sports. As large as football is, National Football League players comprise a small subset of the population who have the athleticism, smarts, skills, and ability to reach professional status.

A number of these individuals began playing football as young children and strengthened their skills with continual practice, coaching, and exposure through high school, college, and into the professional arena. As they excelled, many of their peers who had a passion for football but did not have the skills nor luck to continue moving forward were left behind. Those prior athletes join the rest of us who love football, but have kept our day jobs.

Fantasy football can provide an escape from our daily lives. The last few years have seen a depressed job market, foreclosures hitting record numbers, a country at war, and an increase in high-profile murders and suicides changing our psychological landscape. The result has been people working harder to keep their jobs and spending less on perceived frivolous social activities. Couple this with increased technological advances that limit the need to have in-person contact and we have established a society that can be reliant solely on technology to replace personal interactions.

In fantasy football, you can be alone in your home, but have the satisfaction of being part of a team. You have people to share a common interest and who frequently will ask questions about your mental state if your roster does not look so great. Even if someone does not have 10 to 12 friends to start a league, it is easy to join on the Internet and play with people from around the world.

In fantasy football, a person has the chance to excel within the team concept. Acceptance by peers and social interaction are some of our primary drivers beginning in adolescence. From an early age, we seek to fit into the larger group and identify with those who share common interests to create a social circle. As we grow older and leave adolescence behind, the innate urge to find commonality remains, so we seek new experiences to find our social equilibrium.

Fantasy football fills that void by providing an adult-friendly social catalyst and removing the athletic requirement. In fact, being a strong athlete does not mean you will be a strong fantasy owner. If I spend four months preparing for the fantasy draft, watch the NFL draft, read commentary, review depth charts, and analyze the statistics, I have as good a chance to win as anyone else. If you think about it, how often is our chance to succeed—in anything—equal?

Girls of the gridiron

Considering the concept of equality highlights the absence of women from activities around the NFL. One watching football will not see women on the sidelines (except perhaps as scantily-clad cheerleaders) or in the broadcast booth. There may be a token female reporter—who inevitably is a knockout—giving live "updates" and asking questions at halftime, but none who actively are engaged in the sport.

Women generally show up during a football game sitting next to an owner or kissing their quarterback husband after he helps his team win the Super Bowl. Fantasy football levels the playing field, pun intended. Man or woman, athlete or novice, we all have a chance to win based on our individual efforts. This especially can be appealing for a demographic feeling underrepresented or not included in what can be considered "America's Game."

To excel in this version of football, an individual can draw upon his or her mental knowledge over physical durability.

An ability to engage in football was my earliest draw to begin playing fantasy football eight years ago. I grew up watching the sport with my father and that continued to be all I could do, watch. It is encouraging now to see girls playing on high school teams and engaging in coed flag football leagues. I applaud them all from the sidelines, since I am part of the demographic that was not favored with athletic genes, but I sure do love football. Fantasy football allows me and thousands of others to be part of the game and engage in activities previously reserved for the "boys club."

I still chuckle at the expressions of men who are shocked I know anything about fantasy let alone am checking my scores during the games. I many times have been the only woman in my fantasy league, having been told, "We've never had a girl play before." Remember, success is not determined by gender, speed, or athleticism.

To excel in this version of football, an individual can draw upon his or her mental knowledge over physical durability. This shift in requirement makes the sport more inclusive to those who do not possess the physical stature to reach the professional level. The stereotype of an average fantasy football "player" is an overweight male who sits in front of his computer and never has set foot on a football field. That is the problem with stereotypes; they become exclusive exaggerated representations of a group of people.

Those who play fantasy football represent the diversity within our society. Any individual of any age, sex, creed, and color can play and have a good time, even without really knowing what they are doing. By joining the game, they become part of a larger conversation that now dominates alongside pro football games.

Although it is inclusive, fantasy football still is a gamble. Some leagues charge thousands of dollars to join and the impulse to continue chasing the high of the win now mirrors any other addictive behavior. If we follow the premise that fantasy football allows an escape from our lives, we need to consider what are we escaping to. Does a win in fantasy football mean you are a better person? Are you greeted with cheers every time you leave for work by thousands of individuals screaming your name? Likely not. If this is possible for the winner in your league however, please invite me to your next draft.

If winning fantasy does not change the overall trajectory of your life, then it can be filling a need on a daily basis. I will offer the disclaimer that not everyone who participates in fantasy will become addicted or is using fantasy football as an escape from real life. For some, though, like any other addiction, moderation is not possible. Consider the suggested roots of popularity: money and inclusion with peers. If an individual is experiencing an absence of either, they may look to fill that void with anything that provides relief, albeit temporarily.

Interestingly, fantasy football overlaps with the time of year with general increases in depressive symptoms. The fall and winter bring lowered temperatures and less sunlight—and transitions back to school and a lengthy holiday season. These conditions are prime for an individual to feel isolated, lonely, and not part of the larger societal system. Making the choice to engage in a sport, even from the sidelines, can be the first step in making changes for yourself.

Organizations to Contact

The editors have compiled the following list of organizations concerned with the issues debated in this book. The descriptions are derived from materials provided by the organizations. All have publications or information available for interested readers. The list was compiled on the date of publication of the present volume; the information provided here may change. Be aware that many organizations take several weeks or longer to respond to inquiries, so allow as much time as possible.

American Civil Liberties Union (ACLU)
125 Broad St., 18th Floor, New York, NY   10004
(212) 549-2500
website: www.aclu.org

The American Civil Liberties Union (ACLU) is an organization that works to protect and extend the rights of all Americans, particularly First Amendment rights, equal protection under the law, the right to due process, and the right to privacy. The ACLU fights against the thorniest issues such as racism, sexism, homophobia, religious intolerance, and censorship. However, the organization defends individuals and businesses who voice controversial opinions from censorship and values the right of free speech in public, on television and radio, in print, and on the Internet. On its website, the ACLU posts videos, podcasts, games, documents, reports, and speech transcripts, as well as news and commentary on censorship and free speech issues. It also offers a blog and in-depth reports on related issues.

National Congress of American Indians (NCAI)
1516 P St. NW, Washington, DC   20005
(202) 466-7767 • fax: (202) 466-7797
e-mail: NCAIpress@ncai.org
website: www.ncai.org

The National Congress of American Indians (NCAI) is an indigenous rights organization comprised of formally recognized Indian tribes. It has long opposed derogatory and harmful stereotypes of Native American people in media and popular culture, including their use as sports mascots. NCAI has been working for nearly fifty years to change the name of Washington's NFL team. The group's website features a wide variety of material related to that issue, including news updates, FAQs, position statements, and more.

National Football League (NFL)
345 Park Ave., New York, NY   10017
(212) 450-2000
website: www.nfl.com

The National Football League (NFL) is the premier professional league for football in the United States. The league consists of thirty-two teams split between two conferences—the American Football Conference (AFC) and the National Football Conference (NFC). The NFL performs myriad tasks such as scheduling and coordinating preseason, regular season, and playoff games; formulating, monitoring, and enforcing rules and setting policy; negotiating contracts with television, radio, and other media outlets for the broadcast of games; licensing and merchandising products; and working closely with team owners on a wide range of issues. The NFL website offers information on players, teams, fantasy football, and league history as well as featuring podcasts, videos, blogs, and many other interactive options. The site provides a community for NFL fans to discuss teams, players, and plays in fan forums.

National Football League Alumni Association (NFLAA)
8000 Midlantic Dr., Suite 130 South, Mount Laurel, NJ   08054
(877) 258-6635 • fax: (862) 772-0277
e-mail: memberservice@nflalumni.org
website: www.nflalumni.org

The National Football League Alumni Association (NFLAA) is a nonprofit service organization of former professional football players who volunteer on behalf of youth and charity. The

NFL Alumni's mission is to help members enrich their post-NFL lives through community service. The organization's website features news about former players and their activities, events of interest to football fans, and details about upcoming fundraisers and public appearances by former players.

National Football League Players Association (NFLPA)
2021 L St. NW, Washington, DC 20036
(202) 463-2200
e-mail: mike.donnelly@nflpa.com
website: www.nflplayers.com

The National Football League Players Association (NFLPA) acts as the labor union for the players of the National Football League (NFL), representing players in all negotiations regarding the collective bargaining agreement and monitoring retirement and insurance benefits. The issue of head injuries and concussions is very important to the NFLPA, and the organization lobbies for more research and better policies for players when it comes to injuries. The NFLPA also protects the rights of players by appealing disciplinary measures imposed by the NFL and promotes the image of players across the league through public relations campaigns. The NFLPA website offers a wealth of photos, statistics on individual players, videos, blogs, and the latest news from the NFL.

NOMORE.org
e-mail: http://nomore.org/contact/general-inquiries
website: http://nomore.org

NOMORE.org is a public awareness organization focused on ending domestic violence and sexual assault. The group's mission is to increase visibility and foster dialogue, break social stigma, normalize the conversation around domestic violence and sexual assault, and increase resources to address these issues. The group created groundbreaking public service announcements on domestic violence that aired during NFL games beginning in fall 2014. Nearly two dozen current and former NFL players participated in making the ads. The group aired the first-ever Super Bowl commercial addressing domestic violence and sexual assault in 2015. The NOMORE.org website features information about the group's efforts and offers opportunities for individuals to get involved.

Retired Players Association (RPA)

PO Box 3869, Minneapolis, MN   55403-0869
(952) 923-7509
website: www.nflretiredplayersassociation.org

The Retired Players Association (RPA) is dedicated to providing national advocacy and support for retired professional football players, their families, and the community at large. The RPA's specific area of focus is to raise awareness and funding in support of medical research in the areas of Alzheimer's and amyotrophic lateral sclerosis (ALS), particularly as it relates to repeated head trauma. The RPA provides medical and financial assistance for members suffering from these illnesses. Additionally, the RPA lobbies nationally for more comprehensive medical benefits for retired athletes. The group's website features a variety of news articles and videos about retired players and the group's activities, as well as a wide variety of player-related health resources.

Sports Legacy Institute (SLI)

230 Second Ave., Suite 200, Waltham, MA   02451
(781) 790-1921 • fax: (781) 790-8922
e-mail: info@sportslegacy.org
website: www.sportslegacy.org

The Sports Legacy Institute (SLI) is a Boston-based nonprofit whose mission is to advance the study, treatment, and prevention of brain trauma in athletes and other at-risk groups. SLI pursues its mission through education and prevention programs, advocacy, policy development, and support of medical research at the Center for the Study of Traumatic Encephalopathy at Boston University School of Medicine. The organization's website features extensive information about concussions and chronic traumatic encephalopathy (CTE).

Bibliography

Books

Steve Almond | *Against Football: One Fan's Reluctant Manifesto.* New York: Melville House, 2014.

Monte Burke | *4th and Goal: One Man's Quest to Recapture His Dream.* New York: Grand Central, 2012.

Gregg Easterbrook | *The King of Sports: Football's Impact on America.* New York: St. Martin's Press, 2013.

Mark Edmundson | *Why Football Matters: My Education in the Game.* New York: Penguin, 2014

Mark Fainaru-Wada and Steve Fainaru | *League of Denial: The NFL, Concussions, and the Battle for Truth.* New York: Three Rivers, 2014.

James Holstein | *Is There Life after Football? Surviving the NFL.* New York: New York University Press, 2015.

Jackson Michael | *The Game Before the Money: Voices of the Men Who Built the NFL.* Lincoln: University of Nebraska Press, 2014.

John Schulian, ed. | *Football: Great Writing About the National Sport.* New York: Library of America, 2014.

Periodicals and Internet Sources

Steve Almasy "Judge Approves NFL Concussion Lawsuit Settlement," CNN, April 22, 2015. www.cnn.com.

Associated Press "Ex-Players: NFL Illegally Used Drugs," ESPN, May 22, 2014. http://espn.go.com.

Associated Press "Goodell Defends NFL Policies on Head Injuries to Congress," NFL.com, October 28, 2009. www.nfl.com.

George Attalah and Eric Winston "2015 NFLPA Super Bowl Press Conference Transcript," National Football League Players Association, January 31, 2015. https://nflpa.com.

Allen Barra "Why Don't More People Care If NFL Players Dope?," *The Atlantic*, February 11, 2013.

Ken Belson "Brain Trauma to Affect One in Three Players, NFL Agrees," *New York Times*, September 12, 2014.

Cindy Boren "Does the NFL Have a Women Problem?," *Washington Post*, July 24, 2014.

Matt Bowen "Bounties Part of Game Across the NFL," *Chicago Tribune*, March 2, 2012.

Frances Bridges   "The NFL and Domestic Violence: Impact of Efforts Is to Be Determined," *Forbes*, January 31, 2015.

Bill Briggs   "Legal Procedure: Critics Cry Foul as NFL Defends Nonprofit Status," CNBC, October 28, 2013. www.cnbc.com.

Clifton Brown   "NFL Concussion Conundrum: Can Safety, Violence Co-exist? Challenge Is Daunting," *Sporting News*, May 8, 2012. www.sportingnews.com.

Monte Burke   "Why Is Football So Popular?," *Forbes*, October 9, 2012.

Business Insurance   "Insurers, Fans Expected to Kick in for NFL Settlements; Details of Concussion Deal Could Affect Painkiller Suits," August 18, 2014.

Linda Cottler et al.   "Injury, Pain, and Prescription Opioid Use Among Former National Football League (NFL) Players," *Drug and Alcohol Dependence*, January 28, 2011. www.ncbi.nlm.nih.gov.

Daniel D'Addario   "How the Super Bowl Became Pop's Biggest Stage," *Time*, February 2, 2015.

MaryClaire Dale   "NFL: Nearly 3 in 10 Ex-Players Will Face Alzheimer's, Dementia or Other Neurological Problems," Associated Press, September 12, 2014. http://bigstory.ap.org.

Jack Dickey   "The Performance-Enhancing Drug
                          That Doesn't Enhance Performance,"
                          Slate, November 29, 2012.
                          www.slate.com.

Economist   "The End Zone; Lexington," January
                          31, 2015.

Bob Egelko   "Bill to Classify Cheerleaders as
                          Employees Advances—Stealth 49er
                          Opposition?," *SF Gate* (blog), April 8,
                          2015. http://blog.sfgate.com.

Howard Fendrich   "NFL's Goodell Seeks to Look Past
                          'Tough Year,' to Future," Associated
                          Press, January 30, 2015.
                          http://bigstory.ap.org.

Matt Fitzgerald   "Josh Gordon Suspended at Least 1
                          Year: Latest Details, Comments and
                          Reaction," *Bleacher Report*, February
                          3, 2015. http://bleacherreport.com.

Glamour   "The NFL Pro Fixing the Ray Rice
                          Problem," December 2014.

Ray Glier   "Glendale Mayor, Experts Say NFL
                          Oversells Economic Benefit of Super
                          Bowl," *Al Jazeera America*, January
                          31, 2015.
                          http://america.aljazeera.com.

David Gold   "The Football Effect: Public Opinion
                          & The NFL," Global Strategy Group,
                          October 10, 2013.
                          http://globalstrategygroup.com.

Ian Gordon   "The NFL's Terrible, Horrible, No
                          Good, Very Bad Year," *Mother Jones*,
                          January 29, 2015.

Wendy Halloran   "Senator Critical of NFL Domestic
                          Violence Spending," *Arizona Republic*,
                          January 30, 2015.

Jason Hanna   "Tom Brady Likely Knew of
                          'Inappropriate Activities,' Deflategate
                          Report Says," CNN, May 6, 2015.
                          www.cnn.com.

Sheena Harrison   "NFL Players Hit League Over Drugs;
                          Many Claim Permanent Injury,
                          Addiction," *Business Insurance*, May
                          26, 2014.

Amanda Hess   "The Cheerleaders Rise Up: NFL
                          Cheerleaders Are Putting Down
                          Their Pom-Poms and Demanding a
                          Better Deal," *Slate*, April 23, 2014.
                          www.slate.com.

Melanie Hicken   "The High Cost of Being a Football
                          Fan," CNN/Money, September 7,
                          2013. http://money.cnn.com.

Chris Isidore   "NFL Earns Record Profits Despite
                          Ugly Image," CNN/Money, January
                          20, 2015. http://money.cnn.com.

Chris Isidore   "NFL Gets Billions in Subsidies from
                          US Taxpayers," CNN/Money, January
                          30, 2015. http://money.cnn.com.

Sally Jenkins and Rick Maese	"Federal Drug Agents Launch Surprise Inspections of NFL Teams Following Games," *Washington Post*, November 16, 2014.
Lindsay Jones	"NFL Players Use PSAs to Speak out Against Domestic Abuse," *USA Today*, October 14, 2014.
Tim Kawakami	"49ers Face the Domestic Violence Issue Once Again," *San Jose Mercury News*, March 9, 2015.
Matt Kelly	"NFL Fumbles on Ethical Conduct," *Compliance Week*, October 2014.
Chuck Klosterman	"Hating the Game," *New York Times Magazine*, September 7, 2014.
John Koblinjan	"The Team Behind the NFL's 'No More' Campaign," *New York Times*, January 2, 2015.
Joseph Lapin	"The Public Relations of Brain Injury—How the NFL Hopes to Improve Safety and Their Brand," *Pacific Standard*, December 14, 2012.
Will Leitch	"From Mo'ne Davis to Michael Sam, the Culture Wars Have Invaded the Sports World; Talking Football Is Suddenly a Whole Lot Less Fun," *New York Magazine*, September 8, 2014.

Will Leitch   "Kickoff; All the Things We Won't Be
                     Able to Turn Away from This NFL
                     Season (Despite Our Better
                     Judgment)," *New York Magazine*,
                     August 25, 2014.

Chris McGlynn   "Nothing Is Sacred in Football,"
                     Second Look Sports (blog), February
                     21, 2015. https://secondlooksports
                     .wordpress.com.

Ben McGrath   "Beleaguered League," *New Yorker*,
                     September 29, 2014.

Jane McManus   "Domestic Violence and the NFL:
                     What Impact Has the League Made?,"
                     ESPN, January 28, 2015.
                     http://espn.go.com.

Jane McManus   "When It Comes to Domestic
                     Violence, Heat Is Still on for Roger
                     Goodell," ESPN, January 30, 2015.
                     http://espn.go.com.

Gary Mihoces   "Documentary Says NFL Is a 'League
                     of Denial,'" *USA Today*, October 8,
                     2013.

The Mill   "Super Bowl 2015: Behind NO
                     MORE PSA with NFL's Sam
                     Howard," February 2, 2015.
                     www.themillblog.com.

Joe Mont   "Football Follies: A Study in Ethics
                     and Investigations—NFL in Ethics
                     Tangle After Player Is Charged with
                     Domestic Violence," *Compliance
                     Week*, November 2014.

Benjamin Morris   "The Rate of Domestic Violence
                    Arrests Among NFL Players,"
                    fivethirtyeight.com, July 31, 2014.
                    http://fivethirtyeight.com.

Geoffrey Norman   "The Rise (and Fall?) of the NFL;
                    There Were Giants in the Earth in
                    Those Days . . . and Colts," *Weekly
                    Standard*, January 19, 2015.

Bennet Omalu,   "The Frontline Interviews: League of
interviewed by   Denial—The NFL's Concussion
Michael Kirk   Crisis," PBS, March 25, 2013.
                    www.pbs.org.

Norm Ornstein   "It's Time for Congress to Treat
                    Football Like the Business It Really
                    Is," *National Journal Daily*, September
                    23, 2014.

National Football   "NFL Owners Endorse New Personal
League   Conduct Policy," nfl.com, December
                    10, 2014. www.nfl.com.

Eddie Pells   "NFL Finds Patriots Employees
                    Probably Deflated Balls," Associated
                    Press, May 6, 2015.
                    http://hosted.ap.org.

Eddie Pells   "NFL Players Use Marijuana to 'Cope
                    with the Pain' as League Drug Rules
                    Draw Scrutiny," *Huffington Post*,
                    August 14, 2014.
                    www.huffingtonpost.com.

Dan Pompei   "The Cost of an NFL Career: Former Players Discuss the Early Retirement Trend," *Bleacher Report*, March 24, 2015. http://bleacherreport.com.

Real Clear Sports   "Players Speak Out Against NFL's Dangerous Hit Rule," October 20, 2010. www.realclearsports.com.

Tim Rohan   "Gamesmanship vs. Cheating: Patriots Scandal Continues Long Debate Over Sports Ethics," *New York Times*, January 23, 2015.

Richard Rubin   "NFL Will End Its Tax-Exempt Status, Goodell Tells Owners," bloomberg.com, April 28, 2015. www.bloomberg.com.

Peter Schmuck   "Deflated Football Controversy Just the Latest Reason to Question Integrity in Sports," *Baltimore Sun*, January 22, 2015.

Sky News   "NFL Champions to Donate Brains to Science," March 4, 2015. http://news.sky.com.

Bob Steer   "NFL Commissioner Roger Goodell Speaks in Canton," *Alliance Review*, February 26, 2015.

Mike Tanier   "This Article Will Keep Michael Sam out of the NFL," *Bleacher Report*, February 13, 2015. http://bleacherreport.com.

Fran Tarkenton   "Football's Bounty Hunters Must Be Clipped," *Wall Street Journal*, March 8, 2012.

Amanda Terkel   "How Washington's Football Team Creates a Hostile Environment for Native American Students," *Huffington Post*, July 22, 2014. www.huffingtonpost.com.

Paul Thelen   "The NFL's Drug Problem: How the League's Drug Policy Is Broken," *Bleacher Report*, May 1, 2013. http://bleacherreport.com.

TMZ Sports   "Ray Rice—Elevator Knockout . . . Fiancee Takes Crushing Punch (video)," YouTube, September 8, 2014. www.youtube.com.

Matt Vasilogambros   "Don't Worry, Marshawn Lynch. You Can Deduct Those NFL Fines from Your Taxes," *National Journal*, January 28, 2015.

Travis Waldron   "California Rep. Introduces Bill to Force NFL to Start Paying Cheerleaders Minimum Wage," *Think Progress*, January 30, 2015. http://thinkprogress.org.

Travis Waldron   "ESPN Quit PBS Concussion Partnership Over 'Sensational,' 'Over The Top' Documentary Trailer," *Think Progress*, August 26, 2013. http://thinkprogress.org.

Travis Waldron   "'Independent' Investigation of Ray
                  Rice Incident Mirrors NFL Talking
                  Points," *Think Progress*, January 8,
                  2015. http://thinkprogress.org.

Tom Watson   "The Real Super Bowl Question:
                  Should The NFL Be a Nonprofit?,"
                  Forbes, January 30, 2014.

Mike Wise   "Roger Goodell, NFL Dropped Ball
                  Throughout Ray Rice Process,"
                  Washington Post, July 29, 2014.

Paul Wiseman   "Football's Back: NFL Is a Key Player
                  in the Economy," *USA Today*,
                  September 9, 2011.
                  http://usatoday30.usatoday.com.

Cyd Zeigler   "One Year Later, Has Michael Sam
                  Been Frozen Out of the NFL?," *Out
                  Sports*, February 8, 2015.
                  www.outsports.com.

Dave Zirin   "Time Is Running Out on the NFL,"
                  Progressive, November 2014.

Index

N

CPSIA information can be obtained
at www.ICGtesting.com
Printed in the USA
FFOW05n1723141215